Vegan
Comfort Foods
from Around the World

D1567449

Low Fat Vegan Chef Presents

Vegan
Comfort Foods
from Around the World

Over 60 Delicious and Satisfying Low-Fat Plant Based Recipes

Veronica Grace

Veronica Grace © 2013 — ALL RIGHTS RESERVED.

No part of this publication may be reproduced or transmitted in any form whatsoever, electronic, or mechanical, including photocopying, recording, or by any informational storage or retrieval system without express written, dated and signed permission from the author.

ISBN: 978-0-9919110-1-1

Published by:
Low Fat Vegan Chef
#1627 246 Stewart Green S.W.
Calgary, Alberta, T3H 3C8
Canada
www.LowFatVeganChef.com

Book Layout and Design
Cover Design
Inanna Arthen (By Light Unseen Media)
inannaarthen.com

Chief Editor / Photographer:
VERONICA GRACE

Editor / Proofreader
CYNTHIA P. COLBY (Creative Communications)
cynthiapcolby@sympatico.ca

Contents

Comfort Food from Europe and Asia 77

Contents

CHAPTER 1
FAQs and Informative Stuff

Why Cook Without Oil?

What makes my approach and my recipes different from other chefs is that *nothing* I make is cooked in oil. There are many reasons for this, but I'll quickly go over a few.

Oil is *100% fat* by calories. It is the most refined form of fat you can eat. It is nutritionally devoid of vitamins, minerals, water and fiber. Similarly, white flour and white sugar are nutritionally *devoid* as well, but oil is over *twice* the calories at a fraction of the volume. Oil is also unable to satiate your appetite. Adding oil to recipes regularly can cause you to eat more calories than necessary without getting that feeling of fullness. Unlike if you were to add a similar amount of calories to your dish by adding some nuts or avocado instead. Whole foods are healthy and satiating, refined ones are not.

These are just some of the reasons why I place oil at the top of my unhealthy foods and condiments list.

A bit of flour or a sprinkle of sugar *once in a while* goes a long way toward improving taste or texture in a recipe, especially when you're just learning to make your own vegan recipes. They won't make you gain weight if you eat them only occasionally in small quantities with whole foods. You can of course tailor these recipes to your tastes and health needs and leave them out as well.

Oil is very high in calories and is easy to overdo. People often drizzle *far* more oil on top of their food or into their skillet than they realize. You'll appreciate a little bit of sweetness in a recipe *much* more than you'll appreciate oiliness or greasiness.

Why We Crave Sweet Things

Many health enthusiasts have been scared away from carbohydrates and naturally sweet foods unnecessarily. Not all sweet foods are unhealthy or unnatural. We seek out sweet foods because the tip of our tongue contains many sensors for sweetness. We also have sensors for salty foods *(which contain minerals)* and bitter foods *(for leafy greens)*. But we don't have censors for fat

and protein *(amino acids)* like a cat or carnivore would. We may like eating fatty snack foods for treats, but they're not our main source of calories as a species. Only when fatty or protein rich foods are combined with salt or sugar, do they become more appetizing. Carbohydrates such as potatoes, sweet potatoes, legumes, grains and fruit should be our main source of calories and not fat-rich foods or oils.

Women often load up on salad at restaurants in an effort to try and lose weight and eat "healthier". However, they're often adding 3-4 ounces of pure fat *(in the form of cream/oil based dressings)* on top of their salad along with chicken, bacon, cheese, avocado and nuts.

When compared to lettuce - which has hardly any calories - these added foods are incredibly rich and high in calories. It weighs you down and prevents weight loss, or causes you to gain weight without knowing why.

When you go out to eat at a restaurant or dine at a friend's house, they probably use **more than enough** oil and fat in their recipes as it is. So you really don't need to use it at home as well. This is why I want to teach you how to cook without oil and thus control how much fat you put into your recipes at home.

If you cut just 2 Tbsp. of oil or butter out of your diet every day that adds up to *240 calories!* Potentially, you could lose 1 lb. every 2 weeks without even trying. That's *24 lbs. a year!* It's that easy for weight to creep up *on,* or slip *off* of you.

Small changes like this help you lose weight and achieve and maintain your goal weight. It helps stop or reverse: diabetes, heart disease and even cancer growth. Low fat plant foods are the key to good health and don't need to be drowned in refined oils to taste delicious.

When it comes to compromises on a whole food diet you're better off with a sprinkle of sugar or a piece of bread once in a while which you'll enjoy and appreciate - instead of oil that you don't even notice, putting weight on you.

For more information on the myths of 'heart healthy' oils and nuts please check out this great DVD *From Oil To Nuts* by R.D. Jeff Novick. Everyone I've shown it to is blown away by the misleading information perpetuated by food lobbies and advertisers.

Another great resource for free nutritional information is Dr. Michael Greger's nutritionfacts.org. It contains many helpful videos and articles that are short and concise. If you have any questions on current research studies and health claims based on published medical journal facts, he's the man to ask.

For more books on the science behind my recommendations for an oil free vegan diet check out the following resources on Amazon:

Preventing and Reversing Heart Disease by Dr. Caldwell Esselstyn

The Starch Solution: Eat The Foods You Love and Lose The Weight For Good by Dr. John McDougall

The McDougall Program For Maximum Weight Loss by Dr. John McDougall

Dr. Dean Ornish's Program For Reversing Heart Disease by Dr. Dean Ornish

Eat To Live by Dr. Joel Fuhrman

Super Immunity by Dr. Joel Fuhrman

Eat For Health: Lose Weight and Keep It Off by Dr. Joel Fuhrman

The China Study by Dr. T Colin Campbell

All of the recipes in this book are designed to be in line with the recommendations of the above doctors. These recipes are oil free, low-fat, whole food, and plant-based to help you achieve your health goals and maintain them for life.

How to Cook Without Oil

There are two ways we can do this:

#1: Sautéing onions and garlic dry in a skillet or wok.

Use a non-stick pan and sauté your onions and garlic dry over medium heat for 5-6 minutes until they are softened and translucent. The moisture produced by the onions sweating will prevent them from sticking and create moisture to 'fry' in. If you're cooking much longer than this you may need to add a little vegetable broth or water. Then add in your veggies and sauces or liquids and continue cooking. It's best to use a decent quality non-stick pan. I've found the cheaper ones just don't stand up to my daily use.

#2: Sautéing onions in vegetable broth in a pot or pan.

I use this second method when cooking soups and stews on the stovetop. Fill a large soup pot with 1 cup of vegetable broth to sauté onions, garlic and veggies for 5-6 minutes before adding in other ingredients.

You lose a little of the onion flavor doing this, but you can easily compensate by using more herbs and seasonings. Anyway you won't miss the taste of *oil* in my recipes!

Ingredients Needed for the Following Recipes

Listed below are all the ingredients needed for the recipes in this book. You'll find I often use the same ingredients in different combinations with different seasonings for simplicity and to be cost effective.

If you're new to vegan cooking, or to cooking in general, you'll find that spices will be your biggest cost. Some are between $3 and $6 each. If you're concerned about cost, flip through the recipes to see which ones you'd like to make first - then see what other recipes use the *same* spices so you can make those too.

I make some of my favorites over and over so I always have a good portion of these ingredients on hand and replace them quickly when I run out. Once your pantry and refrigerator are stocked with the essentials, you'll be able to make any recipe you want from this eBook.

You'll also find many of these same spices used in my *other* books—such as *Comfort Soups To Keep You Warm*. So you'll certainly get your money's worth from them - and *lots* of delicious healthy food as well!

I like to mix traditional and newer or more exotic spices when creating dishes from around the world. I find that oil free and vegan cooking is *vastly* improved when you use good quality fragrant spices and fresh herbs.

I've arranged the ingredients so that the most frequently used items are at the top of each category.

Miscellaneous Dried / Packaged Goods

Vegetable broth *(low sodium like Pacific Natural Foods or homemade)*
Silken tofu *(I use Mori-nu firm)*
Firm tofu *(organic if possible)*
Miso paste *(Genmai brown rice is my favorite)*
Nutritional yeast
Salsa *(mild, look for low sodium)*
Pecans
Tahini *(sesame seed butter)*
White wine *(cooking)*
Light soy sauce *(or GF light tamari sauce)*

Maple syrup
Cranberries, dried *(I prefer the apple juice sweetened ones from the health food store)*
Dried mushrooms
Almond milk *(unsweetened original flavor)*
Blackstrap molasses
Dijon mustard
Raisins
Dates *(such as medjool)*
Red wine *(cooking)*
Cocoa powder

Frozen Items

Spinach
Whole corn kernels

Artichoke hearts *(or use frozen)*

Fresh Produce:

Yellow onions (*cooking onions*)
Sweet onions (*Vidalia, Walla Walla, etc.*)
Garlic
Carrots
Celery
Potatoes (*waxy skinned*)
Yams/sweet potatoes
Baby spinach
Red Bell Pepper (*capsicum*)
Eggplant (*aubergine*)
White mushrooms
Ginger root
Chanterelle or hedgehog mushrooms (*or other gourmet mushrooms*)

Portabella mushrooms
Broccoli
Butternut squash
Cauliflower
Lemons
Limes
Golden (*yellow*) beets
Turnips
Cabbage (*green*)
Ripe tomatoes
Acorn Squash
Lettuce
Avocado
Tamarind (*or tamarind paste*)

Dried Beans/Grains/Legumes
(for GF I recommend Tinkyada noodles):

Black beans
Chickpeas / garbanzo beans
French green lentils (*or brown lentils*)
Cannellini / Great Northern beans
Red lentils
Kidney beans
Cornstarch
Arborio rice (*risotto rice*)
Brown Rice (*short grain*)
Small corn tortillas (*look for oil free, low sodium*)

Noodles (*fettuccini, pasta shells, lasagna, spaghetti, rotini, ziti, macaroni*)
Quinoa
Large wheat tortillas (*or GF, look for oil free, low sodium*)
Burger buns/rolls (*GF if preferred*)
White Flour (*or corn starch or GF flour*)
Wild rice
Bread Crumbs (*GF if preferred*)
Croutons / dried bread cubes (*for stuffing*)
Nacho / tortilla chips (*baked*)
Sushi rice

Canned Goods:

Fire roasted canned tomatoes, diced (*Muir Glen in the US, Aylmer brand at Safeway in Canada*)
Canned tomatoes, diced
Chickpeas / garbanzo beans (*salt-free*)
Black beans (*salt-free*)
Cannellini beans (*salt-free*)
Kidney beans (*salt-free*)

Green Jackfruit (*Arroy-D unripe canned jackfruit is found at Asian markets*)
Light coconut milk (*lowest fat or use carton coconut milk*)
Tomato paste
Whole corn kernels (*unsalted, unsweetened*)
Artichoke hearts (*or use frozen*)
For canned beans I recommend Eden Organics No Salt Added beans

Dried Spices

Herbamare (original) or sea salt
Fresh ground black pepper
Thyme
Bay leaves *(from the Bay laurel tree)*
Sweet Spanish smoked paprika
Roasted / regular cumin
Sugar / sweetener *(your choice of)*
Basil
Herbs de Provence
Rosemary
Roasted / regular coriander

Turmeric
Cinnamon
Cardamom, green *(pods and powder)*
Curry Powder
Chili / Chipotle Chile powder
Parsley flakes
Oregano
Italian seasoning *(or Herbs de Provence)*
Cayenne pepper * optional
Cumin Seeds
Whole Cloves
White pepper

Fresh Herbs:

Thyme
Cilantro / Coriander
Dill
Basil
Parsley *(flat leaf)*

Green or Spring onions / scallions
Rosemary
Oregano
Thai Basil *(available at Asian Markets)*

What is this Ingredient?
Deciphering Different Common Names of Ingredients

Some ingredients go by different names depending on the country you live in. I use only one or two common names in my recipes - those most used in Canada and the United States. If they're named differently in your country, please forgive me.

Here are some examples:

Chickpeas / garbanzo beans - are the same: round legumes with little points on one end. I call them chickpeas in my recipes.

Yams / sweet potatoes / kumara - have a reddish-orange colored skin with an orange interior. Canadians say 'yam' and Americans say 'sweet potato'. Any sweet potato-like root can be called a 'sweet potato' in the USA and this can be confusing. So I use the term 'yam' to specifically refer to the orange variety.

Green onions / spring onions / scallions - are all the same: a small, thin, white young onion with a long, green top. I use the term 'green onion'.

Cilantro / coriander - are the same, fresh: a leafy green herb similar in looks to parsley. I use the term 'ground coriander' for the dried spice of this plant. This is NOT the same as 'coriander flakes'. Don't use *dried* cilantro or coriander *flakes* instead of ground coriander seed if specified.

Red bell peppers / sweet peppers / capsicum - are all the same. I use the term 'red bell' *(for its bell shape)* pepper.

Black beans / black turtle beans - are the same: the small shiny variety. I call them 'black beans'.

Why Do Some Recipes Have Sugar or Sweetener In Them?

Some recipes that use canned tomatoes - or something a little bland or acidic - need a bit of sweetness to balance the flavors. However, this does not mean the recipe will taste sweet like candy. When you add a little sweetness it makes the dish taste less bitter, less spicy, or less salty. You can certainly use fresh vine ripened tomatoes instead of canned ones as they are much more flavorful and will cut down on the acidity of the recipe. Fresh is always best when you can get them.

To make the best tasting recipes you have to balance five different flavors: sweet, salty, tangy, bitter, and spicy. You'll notice that recipes with at least 3 or 4 of these will taste better than one that's predominantly sweet, only salty, only bitter, or only spicy.

Use whatever sweetener you prefer. If you prefer to use vegan ones, get vegan sugar or use maple syrup, brown rice syrup, or agave. I prefer to use any sweeteners except for corn syrup or agave*.

For a 100% natural sweetener: Pit some dates, chop them up and blend with water into a paste or syrup to create a "whole food" natural sweetener. It's whole food because it contains all the fiber without being refined like regular sugar or syrups.

If you're against sugar and sweeteners in general, use sweet root vegetables like carrots and golden beets, when cooking, for their natural sweetness. A completely sugar free diet takes some getting used to, so season your recipes to taste with other spices if desired.

*The reason I don't use agave or stevia in these recipes is that, personally, they don't work for me. Agave gives me instant headaches just like high fructose corn syrup does, and I don't react well to stevia powder either. Looking into how agave is manufactured is quite similar to high fructose corn syrup and I believe it's over marketed as a healthy alternative.

Aren't You Concerned About BPA in *Canned* Goods?

BPA stands for *Bisphenol-A.* It is found in the lining of some canned goods.

The majority of the canned goods I use are packed in 'BPA free' cans. Eden Organics recently switched and their new canned beans are labeled 'BPA free.' You can find them at Whole Foods Markets and local health food stores.

For canned tomatoes, I prefer Muir Glen Organic. They have the best tasting tomatoes

and have just switched to *BPA free* cans as well. You can generally tell your can is *BPA free* when it DOES NOT have a white plastic inside lining. A *BPA free* can usually has a metallic lining.

You can also avoid using cans with *BPA* by using dried beans, making your own vegetable broth, or using fresh or homemade stewed tomatoes. It takes more time, but if you're concerned about *BPA* or other canned food health issues they are good alternatives.

Can I Substitute Fresh Cooked Beans for Canned Beans?

Of course you can! I like making my own beans, but I have listed the amount in cans as well. The amount of fresh beans by cup is approximate. There is slightly less than 2 cups of beans per 15 oz. can, so I rounded up. You'll get a better tasting dish if you make fresh beans, *so I hope you try it!*

The calories calculated in each recipe is based on the canned amount so it will be more if you cook your own beans and put in slightly more.

Can I Substitute Dried Herbs For Fresh Ones?

In many of my recipes I used fresh herbs because these taste best. But sometimes you run out of these and I list some substitutions for dried herbs. The flavor will not be as good, so use dried herbs at your discretion. Generally the substitution is: 1 tsp. of dried herbs for every 1 Tbsp. of fresh.

My favorite fresh herbs are thyme and cilantro *(coriander)*. When they're fresh everything tastes more flavorful with them. I try to keep these on hand all the time. When using hard herbs such as thyme, rosemary and oregano, make sure to remove the leaves from the stem, and chop the leaves a little. This makes it easier to eat as you won't get large pieces of herb in one bite.

How the Nutritional Information Is Calculated In This Book

The nutritional information in this book is calculated by using free online databases such as the ones on Cronometer.com and Sparkpeople.com.

My favorite is Sparkpeople because it tells me the calories, fat, and sodium content in each serving. It also has some great weight loss and measurement tracking tools and best of all - *it's free!*

Visually, my recipes make a lot of food, but the calorie content is quite low. It can be difficult when starting out on a low fat vegan diet, to gauge how much food you need to buy and to eat to feel full and satiated. The calorie count will help you see that the volume of food is quite large but the overall calories are low. If you're still hungry, eat a little bit more.

The vegetable broth used in calculating the nutritional content of these recipes is Pacific Natural Foods Organic Low Sodium Vegetable Broth *(if you don't make your own)* and the LOWER amount of either *Herbamare* or salt suggested in the recipe. For example, when I list 1-1¼ tsp. of *Herbamare* or salt, we used only 1 tsp. to calculate the sodium in the recipe. So, if you're watching your sodium intake, you can use the smaller amount and be aware of how much sodium the recipe contains. If you use more salt the sodium content provided is no longer valid. The sodium count is also higher in regular canned beans and vegetable broth as opposed to the low sodium or salt-free variety.

Use salt at your own discretion. Some people find they need to kick up the amount of salt in their low fat recipes AT FIRST as they're used to eating salty restaurant food and frozen and canned meals. This is especially true in the United States! Restaurant food is far saltier there than *anywhere* else I've eaten around the world.

As you start making more homemade food and using less salt, your taste buds will change. You'll become more sensitive to the taste of salt and need less to enjoy your food. This goes for oil too - you'll also enjoy eating foods without oil after a few weeks.

For good health, don't go over one mg. *(milligram)* of sodium per calorie eaten. So for an 800-calorie meal, no more than 800 mg. of sodium should be consumed. When cooking food with canned and packaged ingredients, it may not be possible to follow these guidelines.

So I also suggest *not to salt while cooking the recipes.* Add a little shake to your individual serving just before eating if you're watching your salt intake. Dr. John McDougall recommends this if you're worried about high blood pressure and dietary sodium. Just use a few shakes. Don't overdo it.

The only exception I find about adding salt when cooking, is for beans. They need a little salt while cooking or they turn out bland—but just a *little!*—or you can add some dried seaweed such as *kombu* for flavor.

The nutritional information I've provided covers: number of servings, calories per serving, total grams of fat, saturated fat, sodium, fiber, carbohydrates, sugars and protein.

Remember, fiber and sugars are part of the carbohydrate quantities in the food. 'Sugars' means natural sugars and added sugars combined.

I'm not including mono-unsaturated fat, poly-unsaturated fat, cholesterol or potassium content as I've found most people don't need this information. All of my recipes are cholesterol free by default as only animal products contain cholesterol - not plants.

If you make any changes to the recipes the nutritional information will not be accurate. If you're concerned about fat or sodium content you should recalculate the numbers using one of the websites I mentioned earlier in this chapter.

Please also note that using online calorie calculators can lead to some errors and I cannot guarantee accuracy for the nutritional content provided in this book. If in doubt, calculate the recipe yourself using the exact ingredients you've used to make it.

Tools Necessary for A Low Fat Vegan Kitchen

A Good Knife

If you don't have a good knife, you don't know what you're missing! For the casual home cook it may not seem like a big deal, but having a decent knife that is sharp *(or that you can sharpen)* is *very* important.

Why? Well first of all, for safety. Some people think it's more dangerous to use very sharp knives, but it's just the opposite actually. If you have a sharp knife, the knife will do the cutting for you. You won't be leaning in and bearing down on the knife to cut through things, potentially causing it to slip or slide on you.

The dangers of using a sharp knife are avoided by using common sense:

- Keep it away from children.
- Don't place it on the counter edge so it drops on the floor and can cut you.
- Keep your fingers tucked in and not splayed out when chopping vegetables.
- Keep your first finger knuckles vertical. Use them to guide your knife strokes.
- Look where you're chopping
- Don't go too fast or get distracted
- Protect your fingers at all times!

I've used regular $40-a-set knives for chopping, but they're so darn heavy and get dull very easily. I had pain in my wrist from the frequent chopping and weight of the knife. So I broke down and got a really good Japanese knife from *Global* that was evenly balanced and lightweight. They make a knife with a high-tech molybdenum/vanadium stainless steel blade. It has a razor sharp edge and a lifetime warranty. I would recommend the 8" Cook's Knife, the 5" Cook's Knife *(for smaller hands)* or the 5¼" Santoku Knife for those who like to rock with their slicing motions. If you pick up one of these amazing knives, you'll want to get the Minosharp Ceramic Wheel Water Sharpener Plus as well to keep them factory sharp every time you use them. This sharpener can be used on all of your knives *(except serrated ones)*. There is a cheaper sharpener, but it is for *Global* knives only.

An Alternative to Expensive Knives

If you want an 'easy to use' and light weight *(inexpensive)* knife set, I suggest the Kai Pure Komachi set. It's only $59.95 for an 8-piece set. I have a few of these knives to supplement my collection because they're affordable and comfortable to use. They have a high carbon steel blade and a non-stick coating.

If you don't want a whole set, I'd recommend the 8" Chef's Knife or the Santoku Knife and the Paring Knife. They're $9.95 each and a really good deal.

The best knife for you is one that you feel comfortable using, and that's light and evenly balanced. This way you don't get wrist pain after chopping veggies for an hour or two.

Cutting Boards

I used to use cheap flexible plastic cutting mats before I invested in some cutting boards. They slid all over the place and were really messy when cutting juicy fruit like watermelon and pineapple. Now I have a basic color-coded thicker plastic set, and one large high-end cutting board I use in food demos. I like the plastic cutting boards because I can designate one for cutting onions and garlic *(my yellow one)* and others for cutting vegetables and fruit. This way, I don't get onion or garlic transfer from my cutting board to my fruits. The Epicurean cutting board is nice because of the large surface area. It also has a little juice trap to prevent messes when cutting juicy produce.

The most important recommendation I can give you is to NEVER use a glass cutting board, especially if you have nice expensive knives. It will totally crush and flatten the edge on them and ruin your knives. Use anything else. Just keep ones for onions and meats away from ones for fruits and veggies, and always wash them well between uses.

Onion Goggles

If you wear contact lenses like me when you cook, you'll have some protection from the strong oils from cutting onions. When I cook with my reading glasses on however, I have a hard time to finish cutting an onion without being blinded by tears.

Getting onion goggles depends on how many onions you cut and if your eyes can make it through a whole onion. I use a pair of these when I don't have my contacts in, or when I've been cutting onions for a while and my contacts start stinging. It's worth the $20 to finish your onion chopping with no time wasted on burning eyes.

Another Trick to Prevent Tearing When Cutting Onions

If you don't want to get onion goggles, but you're sensitive to onion oils, you have two options:

Put your onions in the fridge and only take them out when ready to cut. The cold solidifies the oils inside and you can dice 1-1½ onions with little or no problem.

The second option is to use only sweet onions *(like Vidalia or Walla Walla)* because they're much milder and won't cause tearing. I can generally cut up a whole sweet onion with no problem. *(You can put these in the fridge too.)*

Blenders / Food Processors

For some of the recipes in this book you need a good blender or food processor. Get one that's big enough for the job. *Blendtec* is a good choice and you can get it here. I use a *Vitamix* since I make raw food recipes as well and I found it a good investment.

Is There a 'Cheaper' Heavy Duty Blender Available?

For something a bit more heavy duty than a regular blender, but cheaper than a *Vitamix*, I recommend the Omni Power Blender. It costs around $250 USD plus shipping *(half of the price of a Vitamix)*.

Vegetable Slicers / Choppers

The Progressive International Fruit and Vegetable Chopper is a great time saving tool I *can't* live without. I've been using it since I started making raw blended soups. It's handy if your knife skills are lacking. I use it in my raw and cooked vegan recipes for evenly sized, diced veggies for soup, stews and salsas, as well as for home fries, hash browns, and more. For any of my recipes that need a small even dice, I use this as it looks nicer in photos.

Garlic / Ginger Mini Chopper

Peeling and chopping garlic may be the bane of your existence if you can't do it quickly and efficiently. If you use garlic regularly I recommend buying fresh, peeled garlic from the grocery store in a container. For occasional users, smash the garlic clove with the flat side of your knife - lie the knife sideways on top of the clove, then hit the flat side of the blade with your hand. Then peel it. I use the Oxo Good Grips Mini Chopper every day for mincing garlic and ginger. Nothing does it faster, and I hate hand-mincing garlic. You can also use a garlic press. I don't use jars of pre-minced garlic as I find they taste more like preservatives than garlic.

Pressure Cooker

A pressure cooker is an invaluable tool for making healthy, homemade vegan stock, soup, beans, grains and potatoes. It saves so much time and hassle when you cook.

I've used the stovetop Presto 6 Quart Pressure Cooker on my gas stove as well as the Nesco 6 Quart Digital Pressure Cooker that you plug in and set like a rice cooker. I also tried using a stovetop pressure cooker on an electric stove at my mom's place, but it was so difficult to control the heat and keep consistent pressure that I gave up.

My first choice is the electric Nesco 6 Quart Digital Pressure Cooker because it's very safe and easy to use. Just set it and forget it *(as long as you set the valve on the lid to pressurize)*—you can walk away from the kitchen without a worry. It beeps when it's done and you can manually release the pressure or let it depressurize on its own. I bought this while staying at my mom's over the holidays and she was so impressed she's using it regularly. It's great if you're new to cooking and unsure of using a pressure cooker on the stove.

My second choice is a high quality pressure cooker like the Presto 6 Quart Pressure Cooker but only over a gas stove. It's safe and just takes a bit of practice to get the timing and heat correct. It comes with an excellent manual for cooking times, with charts for general guidelines. Practice a few times with water levels and cooking times if using it for whole meals, as gas stoves tend to be hotter and cook faster.

I DO NOT recommend a stove top pressure cooker on an electric stove unless you're skilled and know how to move the pressure cooker from a high heat element to a medium heat element once it's at pressure - or unless you're definite on your cooking times. It takes much longer to heat and come up to pressure, than on a gas stove. I'm not certain how time effective it is for 5-minute recipes like vegetable broth or black beans. Use at your discretion.

What Else Can You Use A Pressure Cooker For?

You can cook all kinds of stuff such as: easy mashed potatoes, dried beans, potato salad, yams, sweet potatoes, stews, cooking whole grains, etc. Electric pressure cookers are a *LIFESAVER* at Thanksgiving, Christmas and Easter when you have a ton of pots on the stove and not a lot of space. You can easily and quickly cook your potatoes or yams in an electric pressure cooker and leave the stove for other things. It's also good for people who don't have a stove and want to make one-pot meals. If that's the case for you, I'd recommend getting an electric rice cooker too.

Slow Cookers or Crock Pots

You'll see some of my recipes with slow cooker directions. Slow cookers are great for making stews and slow cooking beans or grains if you don't have time to watch the stove. Set them on 4 hour and 8 hour cooking times - some also have a 6 hour option or can be programmed for whatever time you desire.

Rice Cookers

I love my *Zojirushi* 5 ½ cup (dry) rice cooker! While the cheap $10 ones might be ok in a pinch, they fail at cooking most things other than plain white rice. If you're interested in cooking whole grains like brown rice or steel cut oats, a better quality rice cooker works wonders. *Zojirushi* makes a number of rice cookers from small personal ones to ones large enough to feed the whole family. There are different settings for white rice, sushi rice, sweet rice, porridge, and cake. You can also program your rice cooker the night before and fill it with water and steel cut oats for homemade oatmeal every morning. It handles the timing for you, so unlike cheap rice cookers you don't have to keep checking it and pressing the lever back down to continue cooking. It has a smart 'fuzzy logic' computer inside that knows how long to cook each grain and only turns off when it's done. Having a rice cooker makes eating rice at home much easier and saves you from having to cook another side dish on the stove while you prepare your main dish.

Debunking Common Cooking Myths

Here are a few very common cooking myths I want to dispel that some people still believe:

Myth: Adding salt to water makes it boil faster.

Truth: Salt slightly raises the boiling temperature of water - it does not in fact boil *faster* when you add salt. Add salt only when the water is already boiling, if desired, for flavor.

Myth: Cold water boils faster than hot water.

Truth: This is simply not true. Just because there's a greater difference between the starting and ending temperatures, does not mean it takes less time to change to the other. Warm water boils faster than cold water because it takes longer for the cold water molecules to speed up and increase in temperature.

Myth: Putting a lid on a pot of water helps it boil faster.

Truth: There is such a slight increase in pressure when covering a pot with a lid that the time saved isn't noticeable. However, don't continue boiling a pot of water or liquids with a lid on. The steam needs to escape and can bubble over if the pressure isn't released. Only cover pots that are on medium low to low heat.

Myth: Salting beans before they're cooked prevents them from softening

Truth: Many people incorrectly believe that adding some salt or baking soda to their beans before they are finished cooking will keep them hard and prevent them from cooking quickly or at all. This is absolutely not true. Tests have been done using both methods and the only major difference was the unsalted beans fell apart a little more easily and the salted ones kept their skins a little more intact and were salty.

Myth: Adding acids such as tomatoes to beans prevents them from softening

Truth: The only effect acids such as tomatoes have on dried beans while they are cooking is to keep the skins intact. Adding tomatoes to dried beans while cooking does not increase the cooking time necessary.

Myth: You must boil pasta in a massive amount of water for it to cook properly.

Truth: As long as the pasta is fully covered by water and you stir it occasionally it should be fine. The only exceptions to the rule that I have found are large pasta shells need more space or else they get stuck inside each other and large lasagna noodles can get stuck to each other. So for those two use a larger amount of water to boil them in.

CHAPTER 2
Cooking Basic Low Fat Vegan Side Dishes

These cooking instructions and tips are for suitable side dishes to accompany the entrée recipes in this eBook.

How to Cook The Perfect Brown Rice

Stove Top Directions For Brown Rice:

1. Measure out 1/3 cup for a small serving and 1 cup for several servings. You can always make a big batch in advance and reheat it later or use to make rice salad or stuffed vegetables.

2. Place rice in a mesh strainer or a bowl and rinse with cool water to remove any debris and excess starch. Drain.

3. Add rinsed rice to a pot. Then add enough water to equal 1½ times the amount of rice. For 1/3 cup, add ½ cup of water. For 1 cup of rice, add 1½ cups of water.

4. Put the uncovered pot on the stove, turn the heat to high and bring it to a boil.

5. When boiling, turn the heat down to simmer and cover with a lid. If your lid has a hole or steam valve cover it with a cloth. DO NOT PEEK OR OPEN THE LID. Let the rice simmer for about 20 minutes.

6. Turn off the heat and let the rice sit and steam for another 10 minutes.

7. Fluff with a fork and serve.

Rice Cooker Directions for Brown Rice:

1. Measure out rice using the measuring cup that comes with rice cooker. *(This is smaller than standard measuring cups, 1 rice measuring cup yields about ¾ cup in a real measuring cup.)* Usually it's 1/3 cup for a small serving and 1 cup for several servings. You can always make a big batch in advance and reheat it later or use to make rice salad.

2. Place rice in a mesh strainer or in rice cooker pan and rinse with cool water to remove any debris and excess starch. Drain.

3. Add rinsed rice to rice cooker pan and add water to the corresponding water level for brown rice. If your rice cooker pan does not have a brown rice and white rice water line, use 1½ times the amount of rice for water. For example: 1/3 cup of rice will need ½ cup of water. 1 cup of dried brown rice will need 1½ cups of water.

4. Turn rice cooker on and select brown rice setting. If your rice cooker does not have a brown rice setting, select white rice or just 'cook'.

5. Once cooking is complete and the rice cooker is on the 'keep warm' setting, let the rice sit and steam for 5-10 minutes before opening.

6. Fluff with a fork and serve.

Please note that brown rice takes *much* longer to cook than white rice because it's a whole grain. The tough outer shell needs to soak and absorb water slowly to soften.

I suggest setting your rice cooker to cook 1 to 2 hours before your main dish is ready to ensure that the rice is ready on time. For basic rice cookers it's about 1 hour of cook time, for the *Zojirushi* it's about 2 hours because it adds a soaking cycle.

How to Cook Perfect White Basmati *(Indian)* Rice

Long grain Indian Basmati rice is a little different from the typical white rice. It is long and thin and, if cooked properly, can be light and fluffy and delicious. Quite often it can be overcooked and turn out sticky and mushy. Follow these directions for the best white Indian Basmati rice.

Stove top directions for white basmati rice:

1. Measure rice and add to a bowl or mesh strainer. Rinse with cold water 3 times moving the grains around with your hands.

2. Add rice to a bowl and use a 1½:1 ratio of *cold* water to rice for firm rice. Use a 2:1 ratio water to rice for softer rice. Add ½ tsp. of salt for every cup of rice. *(This is optional, it helps the grains stay firmer and not stick together.)* Let the rice sit for 30 minutes to 2 hours. This *also* helps stop the grains from breaking and sticking together.

3. Transfer rice and water to a heavy bottomed pot and cover with a fitted lid. If it has a steam vent cover it with a small cloth.

4. Turn to high heat and bring to a boil.

5. When it's at a rolling boil, turn the heat down to a simmer and cook for 12-14 minutes. DO NOT PEEK OR OPEN THE LID.

6. Turn off the heat and let the rice steam for 5-10 minutes.

7. Fluff with a fork and serve.

Rice cooker directions for white basmati rice:

1. Measure rice and add to a bowl or mesh strainer. Rinse with cold water 3 times moving the grains around with your hands.

2. Add rice to a bowl and soak using a 2:1 ration of cold water to rice. Add ½ tsp. of salt for every cup of rice. *(This is optional, it helps the grains stay firmer and not stick together.)* Let the rice sit for 30 minutes.

3. Transfer rice and soaking water to rice cooker pan and set the white rice/regular cook setting.

4. Allow rice to steam for 5-10 minutes when cooking cycle is complete.

5. Fluff with a fork and serve.

NOTE: For firmer, more al dente rice, at the beginning, just rinse in cold water and skip the soaking time. Combine water and rice in a rice cooker and cook on the white rice/regular cook setting.

For cooking brown basmati rice over the stove, use 2 cups of water for every cup of rice. Bring to a boil and cook it covered over a simmer for 35-40 minutes. Let it stand 10-20 minutes after done cooking to finish steaming.

For brown basmati rice in the rice cooker set it to the brown rice setting.

You can also add any additional Indian spices such as cumin seeds, cardamom pods, mustard seeds, whole cloves, cinnamon sticks, turmeric etc. to the soaking water to flavor your rice.

How to Cook Quinoa Perfectly Every Time

Makes 6 cups *(Perfect for dinner with leftovers or in cold salads)*

Ingredients:

1½ cups dry quinoa *(white or red)*

1½ cups water or vegetable broth *(low sodium or homemade)*

2-3 Tbsp. lemon juice

1 tsp. of salt or *Herbamare* *optional

Fresh ground pepper to taste *optional

Seasonings like parsley flakes *optional

Cooking Basic Low-Fat Vegan Side Dishes

Directions:

This method ensures that your quinoa is light and fluffy and never soggy or overcooked. Make a big batch for dinner and save extra portions for the fridge or freezer—it's easy to reheat. Using less water *(1:1 ratio instead of 2:1)* achieves the best results.

Stove Top Directions For Quinoa:

1. Soak quinoa in a large bowl for 15 minutes in cool water.

2. Using a fine mesh strainer, drain and rinse your quinoa until the water is clear and it's no longer foamy - about a minute or two - then dump it into a pot.

3. Combine rinsed quinoa and water *(1:1 ratio)* in a pot. Add seasonings. Turn on to medium heat.

4. When the quinoa is simmering, cover it, reduce it to low heat and cook for 30-35 minutes.

5. When all the water is absorbed remove the pot from heat. Let sit covered for 5 minutes to finish steaming.

6. Fluff with a fork before serving.

7. Serve and refrigerate any leftovers for another dish or to sprinkle on salads.

NOTE: I found black quinoa was a little crunchy using this method. For black quinoa use a ratio of 1¼ cups water to 1 cup of quinoa so it's moister and softer.

Rice Cooker Directions for Quinoa:

1. Soak quinoa for 15 minutes in cool water.

2. Using a fine mesh strainer, drain and rinse your quinoa until the water is clear and it's no longer foamy - about a minute or two.

3. Combine rinsed quinoa and water (use a 1:1 ratio) in rice cooker pan. Add seasonings if desired.

4. Set to white rice setting and cook.

5. When the cooking cycle is complete, leave it on the keep warm cycle and let it steam with the lid closed for 5-10 minutes. Fluff with a fork before serving.

6. Serve with your favorite entree or vegetables.

How to Bake Potatoes Without Oil

What Potato Do I Use For Baked Potatoes?

Use the dark brown rough skinned russet potatoes you find at the grocery store. They make the best baked potatoes and are also good for mashed potatoes. Don't use the smooth waxy skinned yellow or red potatoes for baked jacket potatoes, these are better suited for potato salad, mini roasted potatoes, steamed or boiled potatoes and used in stews and soups.

Make sure that you select russet potatoes that are about the same size as they will cook evenly and be ready at the same time. If you bake medium and large ones together the large ones will not be done when the medium ones are ready.

Should I Cover My Russet Potato In Tinfoil For Baking?

No. I have no idea why people think they should do this, much less why some grocery stores sell russet potatoes in tinfoil. Maybe if you want to barbecue them and protect them from flames, but when you put tinfoil on you are STEAMING the potato from the inside out and not BAKING it. So it is not going to turn out like a baked potato and be all dry and fluffy inside. It will be more watery and dense like potatoes steamed in water. Bake them uncovered for the best results.

How to Bake a Russet Potato Without Oil

1. Preheat your oven to 400° F/ 205° C *(375° F / 190° C on a convection oven)*

2. Wash your russet potatoes well and cut out any 'eyes' or bad spots on the potatoes.

3. Use a fork and poke a lot of holes all over your potatoes. This stops them from cooking unevenly and possibly exploding in the oven. Which you do *not* want!

4. When your oven is up to temperature, place the potatoes on the rack in the middle of the oven. Leave enough space between them so they are not touching.

5. Bake your potatoes for 50-70 minutes *(depending on size)* and check on them after about 50 or 60 minutes. Using a potholder or oven mitt, gently squeeze the potatoes to see if they have softened. If they seem soft all the way through to the middle they are done. If you're not sure, cut one in half to check. If they need more time, continue baking them, or you can microwave for a few minutes to finish them off if you're in a hurry.

NOTE: Once you know the exact cooking time for your oven and this size of potato, write it down or remember it so you don't have to check and guess next time. Usually they'll be done within 60-70 min.

6. To fluff your potato, make a slit across the top of it. Using potholders or oven mitts gently squeeze the bottom of the potato together, like a crab closing its claws. This pushes the insides up and opens it up for filling. I learned this when I worked in a restaurant and had to plate food.

7. Fill your potato with your seasonings - something healthy and vegan, of course! - and serve.

A giant potato like this becomes my entire meal when served with a side of greens. So this makes it an easy AND very affordable vegan meal!

Time Saving Tip: Bake multiple potatoes and keep them in the fridge for future meals. Reheat them for a quick lunch or use as a side dish the next day.

Topping Suggestions for Baked Potatoes:

Fat free salsa	Fresh chives or green onions *(scallions)*
Tabasco sauce	Nutritional yeast
Hummus *(original/roasted red pepper, low fat. Use oil free or make your own.)*	Fat free vegan queso or cheezy sauce *(both featured in this book)*
Baked beans *(my recipe is awesome on potatoes)*	Steamed veggies like broccoli or kale
Salt and pepper	

How to Cook Dried Pasta

It's best to cook pasta in cold filtered water, as opposed to warm or hot tap water, for the best taste. Although hot water boils faster, it comes from your hot water heater and can taste different from fresh cold water.

1. Fill up a large 5-6 qt. 5-6 L. pot with cool filtered water and bring to a boil. When water is boiling you can add a little salt if desired. *(This is personal preference, omit if you are following a low sodium diet)*

2. Add dried pasta and stir to make sure it doesn't stick.

3. Start timing your pasta when the water comes back to a boil.

4. Stir as necessary to prevent from sticking.

5. When pasta is cooked to desired tenderness turn off heat and pour into a colander to drain. Do not rinse.

6. Toss or top with sauce and serve.

TIP: Pasta will clump if left for more than a few minutes, so use immediately or gently run a little water over it and turn it to break up the pasta clumps.

How Much Does Dried Pasta Yield When Cooked?

1 cup of small dry pasta shapes weighs about 4 oz./113.4 g and will make 2½ cups cooked pasta. Four ounces, or 113.4 grams of pasta noodles—*or a 1-inch round bunch*—will make 2 cups of cooked pasta.

How to Cook Dried Beans

I cook my own beans to get the best taste and because it's less expensive. You're more than welcome to start out using canned beans and venture into cooking your own dried beans at a later time.

For those of you who cook your beans, it's probably because you've gotten hooked on how amazingly delicious—and *cheap*—it is to make your own! I recommend making a big batch if you're going to take the time and effort to cook them yourself. Save the leftovers in containers or bags and freeze them for later. Or make a double batch of your recipe to use the beans up and use them for the week's meals. The best tip I have for flavorful beans *(especially chickpeas and white beans)* is to use a bay leaf and some seaweed like *kombu*. When you're not using salt *(or very little)* beans can taste very bland and these seasonings will greatly enhance their flavor.

1. Pick through your dried beans and remove any bits of rocks, broken shells, gross looking beans, random other beans etc.

2. Rinse your beans and place into a large bowl or container. Add 3 cups of water for every single cup of dried beans. Let the beans soak overnight, or begin first thing in the morning so you can use them for dinner.

NOTE: Soak black 'turtle' beans and white beans for only 4 hours. Chickpeas are fine soaked 4-8 hours, but when I soak them overnight they overcook easily. Anything large like chickpeas/garbanzo beans or kidney beans should be soaked for 8 hours. Try not to soak your beans *more* than 8 hours if leaving them overnight. If you do, cook them over the stove as there's less risk of overcooking as opposed to using a pressure cooker.

3. Drain and rinse the beans again in a colander. If using a pressure cooker, add enough water to just cover the beans. Add bay leaves/*kombu*/a little salt or baking soda if desired and cook for the recommended time on a pressure cooker timing chart. For black beans it's 2-3 minutes maximum at high pressure and chickpeas around 5-7 minutes at high pressure *(Less if you soaked them for 8+ hours)*. The Ultimate Pressure Cooking Chart (http://fastcooking.ca/pressure_cookers/cooking_times_pressure_cooker.php _) is a good starting point of reference, but I find their times to be a little high for my gas stove pressure cooker. Always start with a lower time the first time.

When pressure cooking, keep it on high heat until it reaches full pressure *(a steady stream of steam coming out)*, then reduce it to medium-medium high heat *(depending how hot your stove is)* and cook

Cooking Basic Low-Fat Vegan Side Dishes

for the time indicated in your manual or the pressure cooking chart. I like to play it safe and cook at least a minute or two less than the charts suggest. Turn off the heat as soon as the timer sounds. Check the beans and see if they're cooked enough.

> NOTE: I *don't* use oil when cooking my beans in a pressure cooker. Most companies recommend you do so you don't have bean foam clogging up the pressure release valve and make a mess.
>
> To alleviate this problem, I use the *'Quick Release Method.'* I turn off the heat once the timer goes off, then move the pressure cooker into the sink and run cold water on top of the lid until it cools down and the pressurized release opens. This way I don't get any bean foam coming out or making a mess. This works only for stovetop pressure cookers.
>
> For electric pressure cookers it can be a little trickier. Unplug it and place it in the sink and run cold water on it, or put a towel over the top and let out the pressure that way. There will, however, be bean juice and foam coming out of it to soak your towel.

For most things I let the pressure come down naturally, but when cooking black beans you need to do the quick release method or else they'll be mushy and overcooked. They are very finicky and can only be pressure-cooked 1-3 minutes maximum at high pressure.

When cooking beans on the stovetop, always add 3 cups of water for each 1 cup of beans and bay leaves and/or a *Kombu* seaweed strip. (It is up to you if you'd like to add salt to your beans while soaking and cooking. It does help to keep the skins intact a littlebit more.) Bring water and beans to a boil, and then simmer over medium-medium low heat for 1-2½ hours until they give to pressure. *(It depends on size, small beans cook faster)* Make sure they are not crunchy inside or become too soft and mushy like refried beans. Since each bean has a different size, the cooking times will vary. Baking soda helps keep the skins on beans while pressure-cooking, and keeps black beans from losing their color. This is optional for the stovetop.

Quick Soak Method for Beans

If you forget to soak your beans the night before, or in the morning, and you want to make a recipe that day, use the *Quick Soak Method*:

1. Place your dried beans in a pot and fill with water 3 inches above the beans.

2. Bring to a full boil, then turn off the heat and remove from the stove.

3. Cover and let the beans soak in this hot water for 1 hour.

4. Drain and cook as noted above, and your beans should be similar to beans soaked for 8 hours.

Bean Safety

Red and white kidney beans *(like cannellini),* contain a toxin called lection phytohaemagglutinin and must be boiled for 10 minutes to destroy it, before being reduced to medium low and simmering. NEVER eat undercooked red or white kidney beans. If using a slow cooker, make sure it heats above

176 F/80 C to destroy these toxins. Once they're cooked at high heat they're safe to eat.

From Wikipedia: *"Poisoning can be induced from as few as five raw beans, and symptoms occur within three hours, beginning with nausea, then vomiting, which can be severe and sustained (profuse), followed by diarrhea. Recovery occurs within four or five hours of onset, usually without the need for any medical intervention."*

The side effects of eating undercooked red and kidney beans aren't serious, but I want to keep you healthy and safe.

Additional Tips:

Once your beans are cooked, drain them and use them in a recipe—OR—save them in their cooking water and freeze them in smaller portions.

Bean cooking liquid is *great* served over rice or potatoes *(if it's a little seasoned)* so don't just throw it away.

For the best tasting beans I recommend using two bay leaves, *Kombu* seaweed and then seasoning part way through with a little salt or kelp. If you don't season the beans at all they will taste bland and pasty.

Kombu is available at Asian markets and health food stores beside the *Nori* seaweed. You probably won't find this at a regular grocery store though.

CHAPTER 3
Comfort Food from the Americas

Baked Butternut Squash Mac & Cheezy

This is by far the *BEST* vegan Mac & Cheese I've *ever* had! It's so good that all your vegan and omnivore friends will be *begging* you to make it again and again. Best of all, its very low in fat and much healthier than the classic version.

Serves 6

Ingredients:

½ medium butternut squash *(1-2/3 cups cooked and mashed)*

16 oz. / 454 g package elbow macaroni or spirals *(for GF use Tinkyada brand)*

1 large onion, diced

¼ -½ tsp. salt *optional for pasta

½ - ¾ cup/118-177 mL vegetable broth *(for cooking)*

4 cloves garlic, minced

3 tsp. miso *(Genmai Brown Rice is best, use more if using shiro/white/yellow miso)*

3 cups / 710 mL almond milk *(unsweetened original)*

2 Tbsp. flour or cornstarch

¾ cup nutritional yeast flakes

¼-½ tsp. white pepper

½-1 tsp. smoked Spanish paprika

½- ¾ tsp. salt *optional for sauce*

Topping Ingredients:

2/3 cup *panko* breadcrumbs *(or Gluten Free)*

½ tsp. dried basil

¼ tsp. dried oregano

¼ tsp. smoked paprika

Directions:

1. Peel and cube the butternut squash. Boil the squash in a large pot with water until soft. Or cook in a pressure cooker at high pressure for 5-7 minutes. Drain well. Measure out 1-2/3 cup of mashed squash and set aside. TIP: If your squash is hard to peel or cut pop it in the microwave for 3-4 minutes to soften the skin.

2. In a large pot, bring water to a rolling boil and then add salt. Add pasta and cook 5-7 minutes (about 1-2 minutes less than package instructions), just *before* it is tender. Drain well in a colander and rinse in cold water. Do *not* overcook the pasta.

3. Preheat oven to 350° F/ 177° C.

4. Heat vegetable broth in a large saucepan over medium heat and add the onions and garlic. Cook for 5-6 minutes until tender, adding broth when needed to prevent burning.

5. Add cooked onions and any remaining broth from pan into *Vitamix* or food processor. Add mashed squash, miso and 1 cup of almond milk and blend until combined. Set aside.

6. In the same large saucepan, add 1 cup of the almond milk and when heated through, sprinkle 1 Tbsp. of flour or cornstarch, and whisk together. Add the remaining 1 cup of almond milk and sprinkle in another Tbsp. of flour. Whisk this together fast to combine. It's ok if a few small bits of flour are left.

7. Cook the sauce for a minute or two until hot and quickly add the squash mixture and whisk in. Heat through another minute or two and then add the nutritional yeast and whisk in. Turn heat off and add remaining seasonings, starting with the lower amounts. Taste and add additional seasonings to your liking.

8. Add drained pasta to sauce pot and stir to coat. Spread out in a casserole dish. (If you want to add some vegan cheese like *Daiya* cheese you could layer some in now and mix it in, but I prefer to skip fake cheese to keep my recipes healthier). Sprinkle breadcrumbs evenly over top and then sprinkle basil, oregano and paprika to garnish.

9. Bake for 20-30 minutes just until pasta is tender: 20 minutes if you slightly overcooked your

pasta, 30 minutes if you didn't.

10. Serve with steamed broccoli or a green salad. (I like to serve my baked mac on top of a circle of steamed broccoli for presentation.)

Additional Tips

You can also use frozen, cubed butternut squash and cook it and mash it, or use canned butternut squash. Both are sold at the health food store.

For a "saucier" mac, add another ½ cup of almond milk. I like it a bit drier so it can be removed in squares and served easier.

To obtain the tangy cheezy flavor in this recipe, Genmai brown rice miso is essential. Genmai is the name of the type of miso, not a brand. It is much stronger than white or yellow miso. I have tried using white or yellow miso and the sauce was fairly bland and even with increasing the levels it just didn't turn out the same. I find Genmai miso the best for flavor.

Smoked paprika or Spanish paprika is *much* better than traditional paprika. It lends a nice smoky flavor to this cheesy sauce. McCormick makes one, or you can get it at an ethnic or Indian market.

You can toast the breadcrumbs at the end of baking, by turning it to broil and toasting for 1 to 1 ½ minutes. At 2 minutes the breadcrumbs will burn so please be very careful.

Nutrition Facts: 6 Servings, Amount Per Serving: Calories 453.4 Total Fat 4.0 g Sodium 312.4 mg Total Carbohydrate 89.5 g Dietary Fiber 9.6 g Sugars 1.6 g Protein 20.7 g

Better Than Boston Baked Beans

This recipe *shines* when you make *your own* homemade beans and tomato sauce. Feel free to substitute canned beans in a pinch, but you'll be rewarded if you take the time to make your own!

Serves 12 (side servings)

Ingredients:

1 lb. / 454 g. bag of dried navy beans

12 cloves of garlic, minced

2 medium sweet onions, diced

1 28 oz. / 794 g. can plain tomato sauce or crushed tomatoes

1/2 cup brown sugar

1/2 cup / 118 mL blackstrap molasses

4 tsp. smoked paprika

2 ½ Tbsp. apple cider vinegar

2 tsp. dry mustard powder

3 tsp. roasted cumin

3 tsp. light soy sauce or tamari (*Use gluten free if desired*)

½ tsp. chili powder *optional

Salt and fresh ground pepper to taste

1 cup / 237 mL water

Directions:

1. Soak beans in a large bowl with a generous amount of water for about 8 hours or overnight. Make sure there's enough water as the beans will expand a lot.

2. Drain the beans and transfer them into a large pot filled with water 3 inches above the beans and bring to a boil. Reduce and simmer for 15 min to 30 min. If you didn't soak them overnight and just during the day, you may need to boil them for 30-60 minutes until they have softened in the middle a little.

3. Dry sauté the onions and garlic in a non-stick pan over medium heat for 10 minutes. Add the remaining ingredients, except for the water. Taste and add additional heat, salt and pepper if desired.

4. Preheat oven to 350° F/177° C.

5. Cook tomato sauce for about 10 minutes and then carefully transfer to a *Vitamix* or food processor. Blend mixture until smooth or you can leave it chunky if you like.

6. Pour drained cooked beans into a large lasagna-size casserole pan and cover with sauce. Mix together. Add an additional cup of water and stir.

7. Cover with tinfoil and bake in the oven 2½- 3 hours. Check every hour and stir to prevent any beans sticking to the pan or burning. If the beans aren't done and it's too dry, add another cup of hot water. Don't let your beans dry out as they need liquid to cook and become tender.

8. Remove from the oven and let cool for 10 minutes before serving.

9. Serve with potatoes, toast, rice, etc.

Additional Tips:

To serve the beans on baked jacket potatoes, wash the potatoes, pierce them with a fork and place them in the oven. Remove the tinfoil from the casserole pan and move to the lower oven rack for the last 1½ hours of cooking. This way the potatoes will be ready when your beans are.

You can also substitute four 15 oz. /425 g. cans of navy or white beans for the package of dried beans and follow steps #3-8 only.

Nutrition Facts: 12 Servings, Amount Per Serving: Calories 170.8 Total Fat 0.0 g Saturated Fat 0.0 g Sodium 47.2 mg Total Carbohydrate 49.0 g Dietary Fiber 13.3 g Sugars 15.2 g

Black Bean & Corn Tacos

Nothing satisfies like hearty tacos when you're craving something from south of the border. These are *easy* to whip up if you're short on time and can be garnished with all your favorite Tex-Mex toppings *without* the fat or fuss!

Serves 4

Ingredients

8 cloves of garlic, minced

2½ tsp. roasted cumin

1 Tbsp. maple syrup *optional

½-1 tsp. *Herbamare* or salt

2 15 oz. / 425 g. cans unsalted black beans (*or 4 cups cooked*)

1 15 oz. / 425 g. can of unsalted sweet corn, drained (*or 2 cups frozen corn, cooked and drained*)

½ lime, juiced

Dash of fresh ground pepper

12 small corn tortillas

Directions:

1. Pour a little liquid from the beans into a non-stick pan and heat over medium high heat.

2. When the pan is hot, stir in your garlic, cumin, maple syrup and *Herbamare* or salt. Sauté the garlic for 4-6 minutes, just until softened. Add more bean juice if needed to prevent things from drying out and burning.

3. Add beans and a little of the liquid and heat through. Add the corn and stir gently so as not to break the beans.

4. Add lime juice and taste. Adjust seasonings to taste if desired.

5. Serve with small corn tortillas, salsa and/or guacamole, Tabasco sauce, diced onions and/or diced tomatoes, lettuce and fresh cilantro for garnish.

NOTE: Nutritional info only accounts for ingredients in this recipe and NOT any additional condiments.

Nutrition Facts: 4 Servings (3 tacos), Amount Per Serving: Calories 513.9 Total Fat 6.3 g Saturated Fat 1.1 g Sodium 496.6 mg Total Carbohydrate 94.6 g Dietary Fiber 12.4 g Sugars 7.9 g Protein 20.7 g

Cranberry Apple Pecan Holiday Stuffing

Nothing says 'holidays' more than a savory stuffing! You don't need a turkey to achieve moist, mouth watering stuffing. Apple juice does the trick and soon your whole family will swear this vegan version is *far superior* to traditional stuffing!

Serves 10 *(as a side dish)*

Ingredients:

15 cups / 1185 ml. large cubes of bread	2 apples, diced
¾ cup pecans	3½ cups / 828 mL apple juice, divided
1 cup dried cranberries	½ tsp. cinnamon
1 large onion, diced	1½ Tbsp. fresh thyme, chopped (or 1 ½ tsp. dried)
2 stalks of celery, sliced	
2 cups mushrooms, diced	1½ tsp. crushed dried rosemary
½ cup / 118 mL vegetable broth	½ tsp. dried marjoram

Directions:

1. Preheat oven to 350° F/ 177° C.

2. Place bread cubes on a baking sheet and toast in oven for 10-15 minutes until dry. Check after 10 minutes to prevent burning. Or spread them out on a cookie sheet and let them dry overnight.

3. Soak dried cranberries in 3 cups of apple juice for 30 minutes.

4. Place pecans on a baking sheet in the middle of the oven. Toast at 350° F /175° C for 4-5 minutes. Watch carefully to prevent scorching.

5. Sauté onions, celery and mushrooms in vegetable broth over medium heat for 8-10 minutes until soft.

6. Sauté diced apples in remaining ½ cup apple juice and cinnamon until soft.

7. In a large bowl combine ingredients and mix thoroughly until all the herbs are spread out and the bread is moist. If your bread is still a little dry you can pour some extra apple juice in the bottom of the roasting pan to prevent burning and drying out.

8. Spread out in a large lasagna-size roasting pan. Bake for 45 minutes or until heated through and hot in the middle.

   Nutrition Facts: 10 Servings, Amount Per Serving: Calories 360.4 Total Fat 9.7 g Saturated Fat 1.4 g Sodium 472.0 mg Total Carbohydrate 62.8 g Dietary Fiber 4.4 g Sugars 6.9 g Protein 7.7 g

Easy Cheezy Shells and Broccoli

Sometimes you want a quick *Mac & Cheese* you can whip up for lunch or for hungry little ones. *Skip the guilt* with this *low fat version* featuring fresh broccoli for added nutrition!

Serves 6

Ingredients:

1 lb. / 454 g bag shell pasta *(gluten free if desired)*

½ large crown of broccoli cut into small florets and pieces *(about 2 cups)*

4 cups / 1 qt. / 1 L. almond milk *(unsweetened original)*

1 cup nutritional yeast

4 Tbsp. miso *(Genmai brown rice)*

1 tsp. sugar or sweetener *optional

2 tsp. onion powder

2 tsp. garlic powder

½ tsp. turmeric powder

1 tsp. smoked Spanish paprika

8-10 Tbsp. cornstarch

Herbamare or salt *(as desired)*

Pepper *(as desired)*

Directions:

1. Bring a 5-6 quart/liter pot of water to a boil. Add pasta and cook according to package directions or until al dente - between 9 and 11 minutes.

2. Place broccoli florets into a pot with a steamer basket.

3. In a large saucepan, heat the almond milk over medium heat and whisk in all ingredients except for the cornstarch. Use more almond milk for a thinner sauce. Taste and adjust seasonings if desired.

4. Add the cornstarch a little at a time, whisking briskly. Keep whisking until the cornstarch is well combined and you don't see any white floating pieces. Heat to a gentle boil over medium heat, then reduce heat and cook until sauce is thickened to your liking.

5. Steam the broccoli until *al dente* or desired tenderness, 3-5 minutes. Be careful not to overcook. Time it to be done when your sauce is thickened and pasta is cooked and drained.

6. Pour sauce into large pot and add drained pasta. Cook pasta and sauce together over medium heat for 2-3 minutes until the pasta absorbs some of the flavor of the sauce and is softened to your liking. Add the steamed, drained broccoli pieces and gently stir.

7. Spoon shells and broccoli into bowls and serve.

Variations:

Mix it up and substitute a chunk of cauliflower cut into florets or a diced red pepper for a head of broccoli, then steam as above.

Add some cooked veggie sausage or crumbled veggie patties for a 'Mac and wieners' or 'cheese burger' flavor for kids.

Additional Tips:

Refrigerate leftovers for a quick lunch or snack. Bear in mind that the sauce will thicken quite a bit if refrigerated.

Genmai brown rice miso *(the type, not a brand)* is important in making faux cheese. It is much tangier than white or yellow miso. I find Genmai miso gives the best results. You can buy miso at any health store in the refrigerated soy/fake meat section.

Smoked Spanish paprika is much more flavorful than regular paprika. It has a sweet smoky flavor that adds depth. I like to add this to all of my "cheezy" sauces.

Make sure to use a whisk to eliminate clumps of cornstarch in your sauce. If you do get lumps, pour everything into a blender and blend until smooth. Then reheat until thickened to your liking before pouring over the pasta.

Nutrition Facts: 4 Servings, Amount Per Serving: Calories 443 Total Fat 4.8 g Saturated Fat 0.4 g Sodium 178.2 mg Total Carbohydrate 81.1 g Dietary Fiber 10.1 g Sugars 3 g Protein 23.6 g

Gallo Pinto
(Costa Rican Rice and Beans)

This is a dish I enjoyed many times while living in Costa Rica. I also attempted to make it many times at home as well, but without two key—unhealthy—ingredients: oil and *Salsa Lizano* sauce which contains MSG. Here is my take on a healthier version of Costa Rican rice and beans. This is generally a very seasoned and salty dish as the rice and beans are seasoned separately, so use salt to your desired preference.

NOTE: There are 3 additional recipes after the main recipe, for cooking: the tamarind sauce, the rice, and the black beans.

Serves 4-5

Ingredients:

1 large onion, diced

3 tsp. / 45 ml. garlic, minced

2 red bell peppers, deseeded and diced

Black bean juice—reserved or from can

4 cups / 948 g cooked black beans *(two 15 oz. / 425 g. cans)*

1 cup cilantro, chopped *(1 bunch)*

2 tsp. Better Than Bouillon Vegetable Seasoning or 1 vegetable bouillon cube

5 Tbsp. seasoned tamarind sauce *see below* or 4-5 tbsp. vegan Worcestershire sauce

½ tsp. fresh ground pepper *optional*

½ tsp. Herbamare or salt *optional*

4 cups cooked white rice *(cold and refrigerated)*

Directions:

1. In a large wok, sauté onion, garlic and peppers in black bean juice *(reserved or from can)* for 6-8 minutes until slightly soft. Use vegetable broth if it dries up or add additional black bean juice.

2. Add black beans and seasonings and cook for another 5-6 minutes until the peppers are cooked to your liking. Be careful not to stir too roughly and break the beans.

3. Add the cold rice and gently stir to cover with black bean juice and spices. Do not over stir or you will break the ends of the rice and it will become mushy and sticky. Make sure there's just enough liquid to cook it, Too much will make it too wet, and too little and the rice will burn at the bottom.

Gallo Pinto Seasoned Tamarind Sauce Recipe

Ingredients:

½ cup / 118.5 ml. water

1 tsp. sugar or sweetener of choice

1 tsp. Dijon mustard

2 Tbsp. fresh tamarind *(4 pods, peeled & deseeded)*

1 tsp. apple cider vinegar

¼-½ tsp. fresh ground pepper

¼ tsp. low sodium soy sauce *(or gluten free tamari)*

¼ tsp. celery seed *optional*

2 cloves of garlic

Note: You may be able to find tamarind paste in a jar at the health food store. If so, substitute 1 ½ to 2 tbsp. of tamarind paste for the fresh tamarind.

Directions:

1. Combine ingredients in a *Vitamix* or high-powered blender and blend until combined and tamarind is in smallish pieces. Be careful as the tamarind can be quite tough.

2. Strain tamarind fibers out with a fine mesh strainer or cheesecloth.

3. Use on **Gallo Pinto** or other rice and bean dishes.

Seasoned Rice:

Ingredients:

2 cups regular long grain regular white rice *(such as Mexican, not basmati or jasmine)*

1 small bay leaf

1 tsp. Herbamare or salt *optional

Directions:

1. Combine ingredients in a rice cooker and add water to just before the 2 cups fill line. Use a little less if you like firm rice.

2. If you're using the stove, see package directions for how much water to use and how long to cook. Use a little less water for firmer rice.

3. Cook your rice the day before or in the morning. Once it's done, let it steam 10-15 minutes and then immediately fluff with a fork. Spread out on a tray and let it cool. Store it in the fridge. This prevents it from getting mushy when reheated.

Seasoned Black Beans:

Ingredients:

1 cup uncooked dried black beans, or 2 15 oz. / 425 g cans of black beans

1 bay leaf

2 tsp. *Better Than Bouillon* Vegetable Seasoning *or* 1 vegetable bouillon cube or *Herbamare* or salt *(as desired)*

Directions:

1. If using dried beans soak for 3-4 hours. Do not soak overnight, as they'll absorb too much water and split. Drain and rinse.

2. Cook beans in a pressure cooker with enough water to cover, 2 tsp. of *Better Than Bouillon* vegetable seasoning or *Herbamare*, and a bay leaf for about 1-3 minutes, just until tender—use the quick release method. *(If you don't have a pressure cooker, cook beans and bay leaf over medium low heat for 1½ to 2 hours until done)*

3. Now put your beans and the bean water into a pot on the stove and season with additional spices such as cumin, chili powder etc. if desired for more flavor.

Nutrition Facts: 5 Servings, Amount Per Serving: Calories 413.4 Total Fat 1.4 g Saturated Fat 0.3 g Sodium 668.4 mg Total Carbohydrate 85 g Dietary Fiber 15.3 g Sugars 4.4 g Protein 18.5 g

Garlic Mashed Potatoes with Mushrooms

This is a vegan spin on my Mom's semi-famous mashed potatoes. Normally they were so rich and decadent with margarine, sour cream and cheese we never used gravy in our house. But I wanted to create a *healthier version* for our family at holidays and this is what I came up with. I hope *your* family enjoys it too!

Comfort Foods from the Americas

Serves 5-6

Ingredients:

2.5 lbs. / 1.1 kg. Russet potatoes (4-5 small ones)

1½ cups / 354 ml. low sodium vegetable broth—use less for stove top method

½ lb. / 227 g. mushrooms

1 head / bulb garlic

1 medium onion, diced

1 Tbsp. / 15 ml. light soy sauce (or gluten free tamari)

1 Tbsp. brown sugar

1 Tbsp. water

Herbamare or salt to taste

Fresh ground pepper to taste

Directions:

1. Preheat oven to 400° F / 205° C to roast garlic (see cooking directions at end).

2. Peel and dice potatoes and place in a pressure cooker with the vegetable broth. Cook for 4 minutes. Or, steam them in a steamer basket over a pot on the stove.

3. When potatoes are done in the pressure cooker, cover and set them aside while you cook the mushrooms. For the stove top method, remove the steamer basket, set the potatoes aside and cover them. Drain the water.

4. In a wok or large frying pan, sauté the mushrooms and onions with seasonings over medium heat for 5-6 minutes—until they're soft and the mushrooms shrink.

5. Add mushrooms, onions, and garlic to potatoes. Gently combine and mash. Add vegetable broth if desired to add moisture. (Not necessary if cooked in a pressure cooker.) You can season to taste with Herbamare, or salt and pepper, if desired.

6. Transfer to a dish and keep warm in the oven.

How to Roast Garlic:

1. Preheat oven to 400° F / 205° C

2. Slice off a good chunk off the top of the head/bulb of garlic. Make sure all of the cloves are exposed so you'll be able to get them out.

3. Wrap the garlic bulb in tinfoil and place on a baking sheet - or in a muffin tin if roasting more than one bulb at a time. (You can freeze the roasted garlic for use at a later time) If using a muffin tin, add some water to the muffin holders. This helps moisten your garlic so it'll cook faster.

4. Bake for 35-45 minutes until cloves are soft. They'll be very hot, so use oven mitts when squeezing them gently to see if they're done.

5. Your roasted garlic is ready when it turns a golden brown color and is very soft inside. If it's still white and not fully soft, it's not ready.

6. Unwrap the tinfoil & let garlic cool before touching.

7. Squeeze each bulb of garlic separately, careful to not let the hot garlic burn you, or slip out the bottom. Peel the cloves and remove them one by one if you're stickler for maximizing your garlic output!

Your oil-free roasted garlic can now be used in soups, mashed potatoes, dips, or to spread on bread! Save leftovers in a container in the fridge, or freeze.

Variations:

If you don't want to use roasted garlic, cook a few whole cloves of garlic with the potatoes and mash them in.

Nutrition Facts: 5 Servings, Amount Per Serving: Calories 173.7 Total Fat 0.4 g Saturated Fat 0.1 g Sodium 110.9 mg Total Carbohydrate 39.8 g Dietary Fiber 5.0 g Sugars 6.3 g Protein 5.5 g

Hearty Vegetable Slow Cooker Stew

A classic vegan slow cooker stew is just what you need on those cold, snowy days! This recipe makes *great* leftovers for a healthy lunch or can be served at a winter potluck.

Comfort Foods from the Americas

Serves 6

Ingredients:

8 fresh tomatoes or a 28 oz. / 794 g can

6 dates, pitted or 2 Tbsp. sugar *optional

2 tsp. *Herbs de Provence* (or an Italian herb mix)

1 tsp. smoked chipotle powder *optional

1-1½ tsp. Herbamare or salt or as desired

Fresh ground pepper to taste

1 yam/sweet potato, sliced or diced

10 baby potatoes quartered or 2 medium potatoes cubed

2 golden beets or turnips

3 carrots peeled and chopped

3 stalks of celery, chopped

1 onion, diced

6 cloves of garlic, minced

2 low sodium vegetable bouillon cubes for slow cooker/ or 4 cups / 1 qt. of vegetable broth for stovetop

1 tsp. roasted cumin

Slow Cooker Directions:

1. Blend the tomatoes with the *Herbs de Provence* and dates / sugar. Taste, and add salt, pepper and chipotle as desired.

2. Slice the yams/sweet potatoes so they don't fall apart in the slow cooker. Combine all ingredients in the slow cooker, starting with the carrots at the bottom, then potatoes, beets/ turnips, yam, celery, and onions. Pour the tomato mixture over top.

3. Cook on low for 6-7 hours or high for 5 hours - until the potatoes are done and the vegetables are tender. Taste, and adjust seasonings if desired.

4. Serve & *enjoy!*

Stove Top Directions:

1. Chop your vegetables while the onions and garlic are sautéing in 1 cup of vegetable broth over medium heat. If needed, add a little more broth or water to prevent from drying out.

2. Dice your potatoes smaller than your yams/sweet potatoes as they'll take longer to cook. Dice the beets or turnips the same size as your potatoes. Chop the rest of the veggies and add to the pot when ready. Add the remaining 3 cups of vegetable broth. It doesn't have to cover *all* of the vegetables, just *almost.*

3. Blend tomatoes, seasonings and sugar / dates in blender and add to pot.

4. Cover the pot, bring to a boil, and then reduce to medium heat and cook for 45-55 minutes until the potatoes and beets/turnips are soft.

5. Now you can season to taste using *Herbamare* or salt and pepper. Take a potato masher and roughly mash about ¼ of it to make the broth thicker and it will become chunkier too.

6. Serve & *enjoy!*

Nutrition Facts: 6 Servings, Amount Per Serving: Calories 163.1 Total Fat 0.6 g Saturated Fat 0.1 g Sodium 513.6 mg Total Carbohydrate 37.5 g Dietary Fiber 6.3 g Sugars 9.2 g Protein 3.7 g

Herbed Lentil Loaf

This lentil loaf is *incredibly* savory and delicious! It has even *more* flavor than traditional meat loaf and your family will *love* it! Make 1 pan for dinner and freeze the other for a quick dinner later on. It's best served with miso or brown gravy.

Comfort Foods from the Americas

Serves 8: Makes 2 1-quart (9x5x2) size loaves

Ingredients:

1½ cups French green or brown lentils, rinsed

4 cups / 1 qt. / 1 L vegetable broth (low sodium or homemade)

½ cup / 118 ml. of water (if needed)

2 bay leaves

2 medium onions, diced

6 cloves garlic, minced

2 carrots, grated

2 cups cooked brown rice

5 Tbsp. organic ketchup 2 tbsp. fresh thyme, chiffonade or 2 tsp. dried thyme

3 Tbsp. fresh basil, chiffonade or 3 tsp. dried basil

2 Tbsp. fresh oregano, chiffonade or 2 tsp. dried oregano

1 tsp. smoked paprika *optional

½ - ¾ tsp. Herbamare or salt

¼-½ tsp. fresh ground pepper

Directions:

1. Pre-heat the oven to 350° F/177° C.

2. In a large pot, add lentils and bay leaves to the vegetable broth and bring to a boil. Then, simmer over medium low heat until they're really soft, 30-35 minutes. Stir occasionally and add enough water to keep the lentils covered while cooking. Drain thoroughly and press out any excess liquid through a strainer.

3. Dry sauté the onions and garlic in a non-stick pan over medium heat for 5-6 minutes, or until soft.

4. Combine the onions, garlic, shredded carrots, mashed lentils, rice, salt, ketchup, herbs and spices in a large bowl and mix together.

5. Transfer mixture to a food processor and pulse a few times until the lentils and rice are broken up and more uniform in size. It should look a little like cooked ground beef. (If you don't have a food processor, chop the mixture in small batches with a sharp knife. This helps the loaf stick together and makes it denser)

6. Divide mixture and gently press into two 1-1½ qt. glass loaf pans lightly spritzed with cooking spray. The flattened mixture should be only about 2 inches high. If it's too high it may crumble when you cut it. Or you can press it into one large 2.5 -3 qt. pan and cook it a little longer.

7. Bake for 1 hour until it is set on the top. Allow to cool for 10 minutes and then turn upside down onto a plate. Let cool another 10 minutes and then slice with a sharp knife. You may want to rinse and wipe your knife after every one or two slices. The starch from the rice gets stuck on the knife and makes it harder to cut with. You can put the sliced loaf pieces carefully onto a plate and keep them warm in the oven while you prepare the rest of your meal.

8. Delicious served with my **Miso Tahini** (pg. 132) or **Classic Brown Gravy** (pg. 129).

Additional Tips / Notes:

If you can't find French green lentils, use brown lentils. They'll have a slightly dryer texture. They'll also cook a little faster than French green lentils.

Fresh herbs taste *amazing* in this recipe. If you're not going to use all fresh, I would highly recommend, at the very *least* using fresh basil.

Remove the stems of the herbs and chop the leaves in *chiffonade* or small strips.

If you'd like to use cooked *white* rice instead of brown, feel free to substitute. Make sure the rice is not overcooked or too wet as it can change the texture of the loaf. *Al dente* rice works best.

The loaves cook faster if done in 2 loaf pans as they're smaller and denser and are more likely to stay together.

I ended up with nine 1½-inch slices out of each 2 inch high loaf.

You can easily make 1 loaf for now and cover and freeze the other. Before cooking make sure to defrost it overnight in the refrigerator or by setting it out on the counter for 3 or 4 hours. You can also divide the recipe in half for a smaller portion.

Nutritional Info: 8 Servings, Amount Per Serving: Calories 142.4 Total Fat 0.8 g Saturated Fat 0.2 g Sodium 267.4 mg Total Carbohydrate 28.5 g Dietary Fiber 5.7 g Sugars 3.3 g Protein 5.3 g

Top this delicious Lentil Loaf with Classic Brown Gravy (pg. 129) or Miso Tahini Gravy (pg. 132)

Holiday Stuffed Acorn Squash With Wild Rice, Mushrooms & Cranberries

After watching the *Forks Over Knives* DVD I had a *craving* for stuffed acorn squash. This is what I came up with. It's a *great* entrée to serve at a vegan holiday dinner!

Makes 4 -6 stuffed acorn squash halves

Ingredients:

¾ cup dried brown rice, rinsed and cooked

¼ cup dried wild rice, rinsed and cooked

2-3 cups vegetable broth *(homemade or low sodium), divided*

1/3-1/2 cup dried mushrooms

3 medium or 2 large acorn squash

1 Tbsp. maple syrup or brown sugar

Cooking spray

1 medium onion, finely diced

4 celery stalks, diced

¼ cup dried cranberries *(no sugar added variety or sweetened with apple juice)*

½ -1 tsp. *Herbamare* or salt

½ tsp. pepper

½ pecans, toasted - *see Note*

NOTE: To toast raw pecans, preheat oven to 350° F/177° C. Place pecans on baking sheet and toast for about 4-5 minutes. Watch carefully to prevent burning.

Directions:

1. If using a rice cooker, cook your rice 1 hour before you start making the squash. Rinse rice and place in rice cooker. Fill to appropriate line with vegetable stock, not water. Add chopped and rinsed dried mixed mushrooms. Add a little salt and pepper if desired. Stir to combine and cook on mixed rice/white rice setting (depending what kind of rice cooker you have). Let steam 10 minutes after done cooking and fluff with a fork.

2. Heat the oven to 400° F / 204° C and place a rack in the middle position.

3. Cut squash in half with a sharp knife and de-seed. Make sure to get out all the stringy bits inside.

4. Place the squash -hollow side up - on a baking sheet, and spray some cooking spray lightly on the tops and insides of the squash halves. Brush maple syrup on the tops and insides as well, and season with salt and fresh pepper. Roast in the oven for about 30 minutes, until 'fork tender'.

5. Pour the vegetable broth or water into a pan and when it's hot, add the onion, and celery. Cook this for 5-6 minutes, stirring occasionally, until just softened.

6. Remove from heat and stir in the cooked rice, pecans, and cranberries. Add salt and fresh pepper if desired.

7. Scoop the rice filling into the roasted squash halves (about ¾ cup for each if 4 halves, ½ cup if 6 smaller halves)

8. Continue roasting the squash for 20 to 30 minutes more - until it's completely tender, the edges have started to brown a little, and the filling is hot in the middle.

9. Serve the squash warm, with balsamic vinegar on the side as a dip, and a nice salad.

Nutritional Info: 6 Servings, Amount Per Serving: Calories 238.4 Total Fat 7.7 g Saturated Fat 0.7 g Sodium 205.9 mg Total Carbohydrate 42.5 g Dietary Fiber 6.6 g Sugars 6.5 g Protein 4.4 g

Holiday Yam Pecan Casserole

Try this healthier version at your next holiday dinner. It's simple and easy and *incredibly delicious!*

Serves 6

Ingredients:

3 large yams

1/8 cup / 30 ml. maple syrup

1 Tbsp. brown sugar

½ tsp. *Herbamare*

¼ cup pecan halves

Directions:

1. Preheat oven to 350° F / 177° C. Peel and slice yams into 2 thick slices, so they cook faster.

2. Steam yams or cook in a pressure cooker just until tender. As soon as you can poke through them easily with a fork and break them apart they are done.

3. Drain and turn into a bowl and mash with a potato masher.

4. Add seasonings and stir gently.

5. Pour into a casserole pan, garnish with pecans and keep warm in the oven at 350 degrees for 20-30 minutes until needed.

6. Serve and *enjoy!*

Nutrition Facts: 6 Servings, Amount Per Servings: Calories 133.5 Total Fat 3.5g Saturated Fat 0.3g Sodium 237.7mg Total Carbohydrate 25.4g Dietary Fiber 2.7g Sugars 6.1g Protein 1.7g

Jackfruit Carnitas ('Pulled' Jackfruit Tacos)

These will remind you of Cuban *Carnitas* or pulled pork tacos. Use your favorite salsa to infuse the jackfruit, and make this a savory and spicy dish!

Serves 4

Ingredients:

1 20 oz. / 567 g can green jackfruit in brine *(Arroy - D or other brand)*

1 large sweet onion, sliced thinly

4 large cloves of garlic sliced

1 tsp. chipotle chili powder

1 tsp. smoked Spanish paprika

½ tsp. Frontier Mexican Fiesta powder *optional

¼ tsp. roasted ground cumin

¾ tsp. *Herbamare* or salt *(or less if using salted bouillon)*

½ cup / 118 ml. mild or medium salsa *(Trader Joe's tomatillo & No Name brand mild salsa work well)*

1 cup / 237 ml. vegetable broth *(or bouillon in water) *see NOTE*

1- 1½ cups / 237-355ml. water if needed *see NOTE*

2 Tbsp. maple syrup

12 corn tortillas *(look for oil free low sodium ones)*

NOTE: Check your pressure cooker directions for the number of half cups of water you need for each 5 minutes of cooking time. Make sure the broth / water content is sufficient. Stove top pressure cookers need much more water, while digital electric pressure cookers use a smaller amount; - around only ½ cup of broth / water total. The onions release enough water to keep it from burning.

Pressure Cooker Directions:

1. Drain and rinse the jackfruit and slice very thinly.

2. Place the above ingredients, except for tortillas into a pressure cooker.

3. Pressure cook on high for 25 minutes. Check it at 15 or 20 minutes, if it's your first time cooking over the stove, to ensure there's enough liquid in the bottom. You don't want it to burn, but you need to cook the jackfruit well so it's very tender and has a soft texture like pulled pork. If you use a digital pressure cooker, it should be fine left alone for 25 minutes. Use Quick Release method when done cooking.

4. Serve with your favorite sides like corn tortillas, guacamole, salsa, black beans, refried beans, or rice.

Slow Cooker Directions:

1. Place the ingredients in a slow cooker for 5-6 hours on low, but use only ½ cup broth or water. In the pressure cooker the excess water turns into steam, unlike the slow cooker, which traps in moisture.

Additional Tips:

You will have to go to an Asian market or Amazon.com to get canned green Jackfruit. Make sure it says in brine and not in syrup. You don't want sweetened jackfruit for this dish. I found Arroy-D canned jackfruit in the tiny city of Corpus Christi, Texas so if I can find it there, I'm confidant you can find it in most states and countries.

Nutrition Facts: 4 Servings (3 tacos), Amount Per Serving: Calories 309.7 Total Fat 1.8 g Saturated Fat 0.0 g Sodium 444.2 mg Total Carbohydrate 68.0 g Dietary Fiber 5.4 g Sugars 6.5 g Protein 4.4 g

Portabella Black Bean Burritos

I really *love* burritos, but I find ones served at vegetarian restaurants to be lackluster, and often filled with plain veggies, salsa and rice. I wanted to make a much more *flavorful* recipe and find that marinating Portabella mushrooms *gives this old favorite a new spin!*

Serves 4

Ingredients—Burritos:

2 cloves of garlic, minced

1 15 oz. / 425 g. can black beans *(No Salt)* + the liquid or 1¾ cups cooked black beans *(save 3-4 Tbsp. of the cooking liquid)*

½ tsp. roasted cumin

1/8-¼ tsp. *Herbamare* or salt

1 pinch chipotle or chili powder

1 medium red bell pepper, sliced in long strips

1 small onion, halved and sliced in long strips

2½ cups cooked brown or white rice

2 tsp. lime juice

Fresh ground pepper

6 oz. / 170 g. Portabella mushrooms *(2 mushroom caps)* sliced in ¾" strips

1 cup / 237 mL salsa *(look for low sodium)*

1 cup lettuce, shredded

4 large whole-wheat *(or Gluten Free rice tortillas)*

Ingredients—Mushroom Marinade:

2-3 tsp. rice vinegar

1 Tbsp. water

1½ tsp. light soy sauce *(or gluten free tamari)*

1 tsp. maple syrup or other liquid sweetener

2 cloves of garlic, minced or pressed

¼ tsp. roasted cumin

¼ tsp. onion powder

Sprinkle chipotle powder

Fresh ground pepper

Directions:

1. In a small bowl, combine marinade ingredients and stir. Taste and add additional spices if desired. Using a large Ziploc freezer bag *(or two sandwich bags)* place the sliced mushrooms and marinade in the bag(s) and seal. Marinate mushrooms for 30 minutes to an hour while you prep your other ingredients.

2. In a small pot add a few Tbsp. of water and sauté the garlic for a minute or two. Add the black beans and bean liquid *(if you cooked fresh beans, use 3-4 Tbsp. of the cooking liquid instead)*, and all remaining seasonings except for salsa. Stir and heat through. Taste and add additional seasonings if desired. Cover with a lid and keep warm. Be careful not to overcook the beans.

3. In a wok or large skillet add mushrooms and marinade and sauté over medium heat for 1 minute. Add onions and peppers and stir. Cover with a large lid and steam for 2-4 minutes until vegetables are at desired tenderness.

4. Have your rice ready. Assemble burritos. Lay out a tortilla and fill with ½ cup of rice leaving 3 inches on the left side and 3 inches on the bottom. Push everything into the middle and right side of the burrito. Next lay on some beans and a little liquid if desired on top of the rice. Add the portabellas, peppers, and onions. Top with 3 Tbsp. of salsa, and ¼ of the lettuce. Roll the bottom end of the burrito up and away from you and tuck in the left side. Continue rolling and tucking in the left side until finished. Repeat for remaining burritos.

5. Serve & *enjoy!*

Additional Tips:

Don't add too much rice to your burrito. It makes it hard to roll and will taste dry and boring. The portabellas, peppers, onions and beans give you most of the flavor. Brown rice on its own doesn't have much flavor. You may also use white rice or add seasonings to it as well.

Variations:

To add more flavor to your rice, cook it in low sodium vegetable stock and add some Mexican seasonings.

Try serving these burritos with my *Guacamole* (pg. 126) or *Zesty Queso Sauce* (pg. 138). You can also substitute refried beans for the black beans and season accordingly. The portabella mushrooms can also be used inside fajitas, or cut into cubes for shish kabobs.

Nutrition Facts: 4 Servings (1 burrito), Amount Per Serving: Calories 445.5 Total Fat 4.1 g Saturated Fat 1.1 g Sodium 724.1 mg Total Carbohydrate 92.9 g Dietary Fiber 25.9 g Sugars 4.0 g Protein 11.1 g

Quinoa Bean Slow Cooker Chili

This is my *favorite* vegan chili because there are so many flavors to it! Two types of beans make this extra hearty and the quinoa adds a nice 'meaty' texture. Serve this to your family and *they'll hardly notice* it is vegan or 'healthy'!

Comfort Foods from the Americas

Serves 8

Ingredients:

1 large onion

8 cloves minced garlic

3 cups / 711 ml. vegetable broth (if cooking on stovetop)

1 15 oz. / 425 g can of no-salt sweet corn, drained (or 1 ¾ cups fresh or frozen)

4 stalks of celery, diced

2 carrots, diced

2 medium red bell peppers, diced

2 14.5 oz. / 411 g cans fired roasted diced tomatoes

2 6 oz. / 170 g cans tomato paste

2 15 oz. / 425 g cans black beans, no-salt (or 1 cup dried and soaked)

2 15 oz. / 425 g cans kidney beans, no-salt (or 1 cup dried and soaked)

1 cup quinoa (uncooked)

3 Tbsp. light soy sauce (or gluten free tamari)

3 Tbsp. maple syrup

2 Tbsp. roasted cumin powder

2 tsp. Herbs de Provence (or Italian herb mix)

1 Tbsp. smoked Spanish paprika

1 tsp. chipotle or chili powder (more to taste)

Fresh ground pepper (to taste)

NOTE: Soak dried beans overnight. When drained, add them to the bottom of the slow cooker.

Directions:

1. Rinse the quinoa thoroughly in a mesh metal strainer 3 times until all the 'soapy' suds are gone.

2. Place all ingredients into the slow cooker: carrots on the bottom, then kidney beans, celery, black beans, bell pepper, quinoa, onions, garlic, tomato paste and seasonings on top (except sweetener, soy sauce and black pepper) and cook on high for 4-5 hours or 6 to 7 hours on low. (It takes less time using canned beans, so be careful and don't overcook) The quinoa should fall apart and give a chunky look to the chili.

3. When done, add the remaining ingredients and season to your preferred taste. If you'd like a thinner chili you can add a little bit of water if desired.

4. Now stir in the: maple syrup / sweetener, soy sauce / tamari, and fresh ground pepper. Add more chipotle if desired.

NOTE: When using fresh tomatoes, add a little more cumin or salt to bring out the flavor before serving.

Stove top directions:

1. If using dried beans, soak them overnight and drain them.

2. Sauté onions and garlic in 1 cup vegetable broth in a large pot over medium heat for 5-6 minutes.

3. Add the remaining vegetable broth and the vegetables and sauté for another 3-4 minutes.

4. Add the canned tomatoes, tomato paste and spices and stir.

5. Add the soaked dried beans.

6. Bring to a boil for 2-3 minutes (only boil for 3 minutes if using dried beans) and then reduce to medium low and cover. Stir occasionally. Adjust liquid level with more broth so beans and

vegetables are covered while they simmer.

7. Rinse and soak quinoa for 15 minutes. Drain and place in a medium saucepan with 1 cup of water. Bring to a simmer over medium heat. Reduce to low and cook covered for 30 minutes.

8. When your beans and vegetables are at desired tenderness *(30 min - 1 hour depending on if you use canned beans, or soaked fresh beans)* add the quinoa, soy sauce or tamari and sweetener and then taste test. Season the chili to taste.

9. Serve with your favorite bread or side dish.

Additional Tips:

You can easily freeze any leftovers or use them as quick meals during the week. You can also halve this recipe if you'd like a smaller amount, but I like this double recipe as it fills up my 6 qt. Crock Pot.

I always make this recipe with fresh dried beans. I just soak them the night before and drain in the morning and assemble the chili. To save time you can also measure out and soak beans in advance and then towel dry and freeze them so you have soaked beans whenever you need.

Nutrition Facts: 8 Servings, Amount Per Serving: Calories 441.4 Total Fat 2.9 g Saturated Fat 0.1 g Sodium 282.3 mg Total Carbohydrate 82.8 g Dietary Fiber 18.5 g Sugars 14.1 g Protein 20.1 g

Quinoa growing in Cachilaya, Bolivia. Photo by Michael Hermann, Creative Commons license http://www.cropsforthefuture.org/

Rainbow Nachos

For a *serious* craving for loaded nachos, try out my vibrantly colored bean and veggie packed version! For truly *guilt-free* nachos try using baked tortilla chips, or rice crackers.

Serves 4

Ingredients:

½ cup black beans *(no-salt canned and save the juice or fresh cooked)*

½ cup cooked quinoa

1-2 cloves of garlic, minced

¼ tsp. cumin

Pinch of chipotle powder

Fresh ground pepper to taste

Dash of salt

½ cup sweet corn *(no-salt canned or frozen cooked)*

½ cup red bell pepper, diced

1 green/spring onion, sliced

1 cup / 118 ml. *Zesty Queso Sauce (find in the sauces section)*

5 oz. / 142 g. corn tortilla chips or rice crackers *(preferably baked)*

Directions:

1. Preheat oven to 350° F / 177° C.

2. Heat your **canned* black beans in a small pot using their juice.

3. Season them with garlic, cumin, chipotle, pepper and salt.

4. Cook for a few minutes until the garlic is soft.

5. If using **fresh cooked* black beans, season them while they finish cooking.

6. Portion out ½ cup of beans and drain.

7. Arrange tortilla or rice crackers on a baking sheet or pie pan. Top with quinoa, corn, beans and peppers.

8. Drizzle with *Zesty Queso Sauce* (pg. 138) and bake in the oven until the toppings are hot -about 10 minutes.

9. Remove from oven and garnish with green onion and serve with salsa or guacamole if desired.

Variations:

The topping possibilities are *endless!* Top baked nachos with thinly shredded raw veggies like carrots, red cabbage or red onion.

Instead of red bell peppers, use orange or yellow, or add little cubes of zucchini or summer squash.

Instead of black beans add sautéed mushrooms seasoned with garlic, ginger, and light soy sauce or tamari.

Nutrition Facts: *(including 1 cup Zesty Queso Sauce)* **4 Servings, Amount Per Serving Calories 378.2 Total Fat 5.0 g Saturated Fat 1.0 g Sodium 283.9 mg Total Carbohydrate 64.9 g Dietary Fiber 11.3 g Sugars 2.0 g Protein 23.8 g**

Saucy Eggplant Fajitas

Instead of plain old bell peppers and onions in fajitas *(like many restaurants offer as the 'vegetarian version')* why not mix it up and try something else? These *saucy* eggplant fajitas will become *a new favorite!*

Serves 2

Ingredients:

1 14.5 oz. / 411 g. can fire roasted tomatoes

1 eggplant

1 onion, cut into strips

1-2 red bell peppers *(or color of choice)* cut into strips

1 tsp. sugar or sweetener *optional*

¼ tsp. chipotle chili powder

½ tsp. smoked Spanish paprika

¼ tsp. onion powder

¼ tsp. garlic powder

¼ tsp. roasted cumin

¼ tsp. dried oregano

Salt and pepper to taste

8 soft corn tortillas *(look for oil free, low sodium)*

Directions:

1. Wash eggplant and cut in half. Slice into finger sized spears and set aside.

2. Add tomatoes, onions and eggplant to a large pan and heat over medium heat. Cook for 5 minutes.

3. Add seasonings except for salt and pepper and stir. Add bell peppers and stir. Continue cooking until eggplant softens.

4. Serve in warm corn tortillas with guacamole or **Zesty Queso Sauce.**

Variations:

You can substitute the eggplant with 2 small zucchinis or 2 large portabella mushroom caps sliced into spears for variety.

To make these fajitas spicier add more chipotle or chili powder.

Nutrition Facts: 2 Servings, Amount Per Serving: Calories 414.4 Total Fat 3.4 g Saturated Fat 0.1 g Sodium 390.0 mg Total Carbohydrate 91.0 g Dietary Fiber 19.5 g Sugars 17.6 g Protein 12.6 g

Slow Cooker Meatless Sloppy Joes

I honestly don't know what actually goes into making real *Sloppy Joes* as I've never made them (but I can imagine it's not good). This *healthier vegan version* gives you the same warm, childhood satisfaction of eating a saucy Sloppy Joe— but *without* the guilt *or* the fat!

Serves 8

Ingredients:

2 15 oz. / 425 g. cans no-salt red kidney beans *(or 4 cups fresh cooked)*

2 large onions, sliced and chopped

2 large red bell peppers, sliced and chopped

1 14.5 oz. / 411 g. can fire roasted, crushed tomatoes or tomato sauce

8 cloves of garlic, minced

¼ cup / 60 ml. organic ketchup *(low sodium)*

1 Tbsp. Dijon mustard

½ Tbsp. blackstrap molasses

1 tsp. chipotle or chili powder

½ tsp. roasted cumin

½ tsp. smoked paprika

8 hamburger buns or rolls *(Gluten free if desired)*

Directions:

1. Drain the kidney beans and pour into a shallow dish. Mash them with a potato masher until they're mostly broken up.

2. Arrange the ingredients in the slow cooker starting with the onions, then beans, peppers, tomatoes, with garlic and seasonings on top.

3. Cook on low for 5-6 hours, or high for 3-4 hours. Stir and taste. Add more spices if desired.

4. Serve with large hamburger buns or rolls.

Variations:

This recipe can double as a quick chili. Just add more beans or vegetables and remove the ketchup and mustard.

Additional Tips:

Mash the beans really well as they need to absorb the liquid. If you don't, it'll be too runny.

Nutrition Facts: (Includes bun) 8 Servings, Amount Per Serving: Calories 301.5 Total Fat 2.4 g Saturated Fat 0.0 g Sodium 443.3 mg Total Carbohydrate 58.8 g Dietary Fiber 11.6 g Sugars 9.0 g Protein 13.3 g

Spicy Mexican Black Bean Burgers

These homemade Mexi-burgers *beat frozen ones by a mile* for taste and texture! *Best of all* they are *all natural* and contain only vegetables, beans and grains with *no funny stuff!* Make up a batch of these and freeze the leftovers for an *easy meal.*

Makes 5 patties

Ingredients:

½ cup finely chopped onions (*about ¼ of a large onion*)

½ cup finely chopped carrots (*about 1 medium carrot*)

½ cup corn, no-salt (*frozen or canned, drained*)

½ cup finely chopped portabella mushrooms or brown mushrooms

½ cup / 118 ml vegetable broth (*low sodium*)

5 cloves garlic, minced

5 tablespoons ketchup (*low sodium*)

4 teaspoons Dijon mustard

4 teaspoons roasted cumin powder (*or regular*)

1 teaspoon chipotle chili powder

2 small wedges of lime, juiced

dash of *Herbamare* or salt

1 15 oz/425 g can black beans no-salt, drained (*or about 1 ¾ cups cooked*)

1 cup panko bread crumbs (*or GF bread crumbs*)

Directions:

1. Preheat oven to 450° F / 232 C. In a skillet, sauté onions, carrots, mushrooms and corn in ½ cup vegetable broth over medium heat for 7-8 minutes until softened.

2. Add garlic and cook 1 minute more.

3. Pour vegetables into metal strainer and drain off excess liquid.

4. Pour into a bowl and add the ketchup, *Dijon,* cumin, chipotle powder, lime juice and *Herbamare.* Stir to combine.

5. Place the vegetable mixture into a food processor with the drained black beans and bread crumbs and pulse a few times to combine and break up the beans.

6. Form the mixture into 5 large patties or as desired.

7. Place them on a tin foil-lined baking sheet covered with non stick spray and bake for 15 minutes. Carefully turn over and bake another 5 minutes. Be careful to handle the burgers very gently and only with a sturdy spatula. Place on buns and garnish as desired.

8. Serve and *enjoy!*

Nutrition: 5 Servings (patty only), Amount Per Serving: Calories 167.9 Total Fat 1.3 g Saturated Fat 0.1 g Sodium 289.7 mg Total Carbohydrate 32.4 g Dietary Fiber 5.9 g Sugars 5.8 g Protein 7.9 g

Yam and French Lentil Shepherd's Pie'

Shepherd's Pie, or Cottage Pie, is found in Canada, the United States and the United Kingdom. Typically it was prepared by working class people and made with mutton or lamb and topped with potatoes. My version has a modern spin and is more flavorful. This is one of my *favorite* comfort recipes because it's so savory and filling!

Serves 4

Ingredients:

1 cup lentils, French green or brown *(picked over & rinsed)*

3 bay leaves

2.5 - 3 lbs. / 1.1 kg—1.4 kg white potatoes & yams/sweet potatoes *(about 2 large yams, 2 medium potatoes)*

1 medium onion, minced

2 cloves garlic, minced

1½ cups / 177 mL vegetable broth *(low sodium or homemade)*

½ tsp. roasted cumin

2 Tbsp. organic ketchup

¼ cup / 60 ml. coconut or almond milk

½ tsp. pepper

½ tsp. *Herbamare* or salt (to taste)

1 cob fresh sweet corn *(or 1 cup. frozen or canned corn)*

Directions for Lentils (Pressure Cooker):

1. In a large pressure cooker, add lentils and fill with 1 - 1½ cups of water.

2. Add salt and bay leaves and bring to a boil. Cook with full pressure for 5-7 minutes. *(French green lentils take longer to cook)*

3. When pressure is reached, turn down to medium. Let pressure reduce of its own accord.

Directions for Lentils (Stove Top):

1. Place the lentils in a large pot and fill with water up to 2 inches above them.

2. Add 3 bay leaves and a little salt and cook for 20-25 minutes until lentils are almost done and slightly soft. Continue to step 4.

4. While lentils are cooking, peel yams and potatoes. Cut yams into 1" slices and potatoes into ¾" slices. Yams should be in bigger slices so they don't fall apart.

5. When lentils are done in pressure cooker, drain and set aside.

6. Add potatoes and yams to pressure cooker and fill until just covered with water. Cook potatoes and yams using the same 3 bay leaves and a little salt for 5-6 min.

7. While potatoes are cooking, sauté the onions and garlic in ½ cup vegetable broth for 5 minutes, until translucent. Add lentils, cumin, and ketchup and continue to cook until lentils are soft, about 5 more minutes. Add the rest of the broth to keep from burning. Taste, and add additional salt or pepper if desired.

8. Preheat oven to 375° F / 163° C.

9. Drain the yams and potatoes and mash with a potato masher. Add coconut/almond milk, pepper and *Herbamare* and taste.

10. Pour lentils into the bottom of a pie dish and top with corn, spreading evenly. Scoop mashed potato and yam mixture on top and smooth over.

11. Bake at 375° F / 163° C for 30 minutes until warmed through and corn is soft.

12. Serve & *enjoy!*

NOTE: If you don't have a pressure cooker, boil potatoes and yams with a little salt until tender.

Nutrition Facts: 4 Servings, Amount Per Serving: Calories 448.6 Total Fat 1.1 g Saturated Fat 0.2 g Sodium 341.1 mg Total Carbohydrate 100.5 g Dietary Fiber 16.2 g Sugars 6.4 g Protein 12.0 g

Yam Black Bean Enchiladas

While traveling around Texas I was inspired to make some low fat vegan enchiladas. I think yams and black beans are *so delicious and filling*, you won't even *miss* the cheese in this hearty recipe!

Serves 4: Makes 12 enchiladas

Ingredients for enchiladas:

1 lb. 5 oz. /600 g. yams or sweet potatoes

1 15 oz. / 425 g. can black beans *(salt free or 2 cups cooked)*

3 cloves garlic

½ tsp. roasted cumin

Pinch of *Herbamare* or salt *optional

Fresh ground pepper *(to taste)*

12 small corn tortillas *(look for oil free low sodium ones)*

¾ cup Zesty Queso Sauce

2 green onions, chopped *optional

1 handful of cilantro, chopped *optional

Ingredients for enchilada sauce:

1 medium onion, diced

4 cloves of garlic, minced

2 Tbsp. tomato paste

1 cup water

1 cup mild salsa *(look for low sodium)*

1 cup / 237 mL fire roasted crushed tomatoes

1 tsp. sugar or sweetener *optional

½ tsp. roasted cumin

¼ tsp. chipotle chili powder

Fresh ground pepper

Directions:

1. Preheat oven to 350° F/177° C. Peel yams and slice into rounds. Steam them until they are just tender. Cool and cut into cubes.

3. Heat black beans in a pot over medium heat and add garlic, cumin and *Herbamare* or salt. Set aside.

4. Sauté onions and garlic for enchilada sauce dry in a non-stick pan over medium heat for 5-6 minutes. Add cooked onions and garlic and remaining enchilada sauce ingredients to a blender or *Vitamix* and process until smooth.

5. Assemble enchiladas: take a corn tortilla and fill with yams and black beans and roll so seam is up. Place into a rectangular casserole dish. Continue until all enchiladas are rolled. Top with enchilada sauce and ***Zesty Queso Sauce.***

6. Bake enchiladas for 10 minutes until warm. *(If you bake any longer the corn tortillas will fall apart.)*

7. Plate and garnish with green onions and cilantro if desired.

Nutrition Facts: 4 Servings (inc. Zesty Queso), Amount Per Serving: Calories 465.1 Total Fat 2.4 g Sat. Fat 0.2 g Sodium 724.6 mg Total Carbs 94.3 g Dietary Fiber 20.0 g Sugars 7.6 g Protein 14.5 g

CHAPTER 4
Comfort Foods from Europe and Asia

Baked Spinach and Artichoke Risotto

This baked risotto *removes all the hassle* from stirring traditional risotto. It yields a creamy and decadent dish you'll want to make *again and again*!

Serves 4

Ingredients:

1 large onion, diced

4 cloves garlic, minced

4 Tbsp. fresh thyme, chopped

½ cup/ 118 ml. white wine or cooking wine

1½ cups Arborio rice

2 cups baby spinach, packed

1 14 oz. / 397g. Jar of artichoke hearts *(in water)* drained *(or about 8 oz. frozen)*

4 cups / 1 quart/1 L vegetable broth *(low sodium or homemade)*

2 Tbsp. lemon juice

1½ tsp. *Herbamare* or salt

¼ tsp. Fresh ground pepper

NOTE: Arborio rice is essential for making risotto. Do NOT substitute regular white rice or brown rice. Risotto is a very creamy dish due to the high starch content of Arborio rice. Look for it in the Italian/Mediterranean section of your grocery store.

Directions:

1. In a large non-stick wok or frying pan dry sauté onion and garlic over medium heat for 5-6 minutes.

2. Add the fresh thyme, white wine, and Arborio rice and sauté for 2 more minutes.

3. Add the spinach and cook until wilted. Remove from heat.

4. Transfer contents into a deep casserole dish.

5. Slice the artichoke heart into bite sized pieces. Add vegetable broth, lemon juice, and artichoke hearts to the casserole dish. Stir and cover with tinfoil or a lid.

6. Bake at 375° F / 163° C for 45 minutes. Stir half way through cooking.

7. If you still have a lot of liquid, uncover the rice and continue cooking. If you don't, have a lot of liquid left, leave it covered.

8. Remove risotto from oven and season with salt and pepper. Cover and let stand 5 minutes.

9. Serve immediately & *enjoy!*

Nutrition Facts: 4 Servings, Amount Per Serving: Calories 319.5 Total Fat 0.1 g Saturated Fat 0.0 g Sodium 366.0 mg Total Carbohydrate 64.1 g Dietary Fiber 3.8 g Sugars 2.5 g Protein 5.5 g

Baked Ziti with Greens

Baked Ziti is much *faster* to make than lasagna and *just* as hearty, satisfying, and impressive!

Serves 6

Ingredients:

1 lb. / 454 g. tube-shaped pasta like ziti, penne, rigatoni etc. *(Use GF or WW if desired)*

2-4 cups packed baby spinach or other greens chopped into bite-sized pieces

Ingredients for Sauce:

1 onion, diced

10 cloves of garlic

2 28 oz. / 793 g. cans of fire roasted crushed or diced tomatoes

1 tsp. sugar or sweetener *optional*

½ tsp. Herbamare or salt

¼ tsp. fresh ground pepper

¾ tsp. basil

¾ tsp. oregano

Ingredients for Tofu Ricotta:

2 12.3 oz. / 349 g. packages of silken firm tofu, drained *(mori-nu)*

8-10 cloves of garlic

1/3 cup nutritional yeast

2½ Tbsp. miso *(Genmai brown rice)*

1 Tbsp. lemon juice

1 tsp. maple syrup or liquid sweetener

Directions:

1. In a 5-6 qt./ 5-6 L. pot bring water to a boil and add salt if desired. Cook pasta until *al dente—* or 1 minute less than the package suggests. Drain and rinse if desired. Try not to overcook the pasta or the tubes will collapse.

2. Preheat oven to 375° F / 163° C. *(While the pasta water is boiling you can start the sauce.)* In a large non-stick pan, sauté the onions dry over medium heat for 6-7 minutes, until translucent. Add the minced garlic. Stir occasionally so it doesn't burn. Add a little vegetable broth or water if necessary to prevent burning. Add the canned tomatoes and seasonings. Taste and adjust seasonings if desired. Pour mixture into a *Vitamix* or blender. You may have to do it in two batches. Blend until smooth and then return to the pan to keep warm.

3. In a medium-sized bowl, crumble silken tofu and add seasonings. Mix with a wooden spoon or fork to break up the miso so it's distributed evenly. Taste and adjust seasonings if desired.

4. When pasta is ready and drained *(try not to let it sit and cool too long)* toss it in large bowl with the tofu ricotta. Mix gently to ensure the pasta doesn't break.

5. Pour half of the pasta mixture into a 4.5 qt. casserole pan. Pour half of the sauce over it and then lay the chopped spinach down. Pour the remaining pasta over it, spread it out evenly and top with remaining sauce. Garnish with nutritional yeast or dried basil if desired.

6. Bake uncovered for 30-45 minutes until very warm in the center, and the pasta is cooked to your desired tenderness.

7. Before serving, let cool for 5-10 minutes to let the sauce thicken so it's easier to slice out of the pan and serve.

Variations:

If you want a stronger green than the spinach would normally have, chop and blanch the leaves in boiling water or steam for 2-3 minutes and drain. Don't use raw kale, collards or turnip greens. They won't have enough time to cook in the oven.

You can also add roasted or sautéed eggplant, zucchini, mushrooms etc. to this dish for more variety.

Try different sized tube pasta to get a different texture / look for this casserole.

Nutrition Facts: 6 Servings, Amount Per Serving: Calories 482.1 Total Fat 5.1 g Saturated Fat 0.7 g Sodium 786.4 mg Total Carbohydrate 81.9 g Dietary Fiber 7.8 g Sugars 14.1 g Protein 24.9 g

The Best Cabbage Rolls

I tested different variations of this recipe *several times* until I found the *perfect* mixture for the filling! Even those who aren't already a fan of cabbage rolls will *devour* these and *ask for more!*

Serves 6 - Makes 12-14 rolls

Ingredients:

1 large head of green cabbage

1½ cups white beans cooked (*1/2 cup dried or almost 1 can*)

1 cup French green lentils cooked (*1/2 cup dried, or ½ can*)

6 bay leaves

1 cup cooked brown rice

¾ of a medium red onion, minced

4 cloves of garlic minced

2 tsp. fresh basil, minced (*or 1 tsp. dried*)

1 sprig of fresh thyme with leaves removed

½ tsp. *Herbamare* or salt

¾ tsp. fresh ground pepper

Ingredients for Sauce:

4 cups / 32 oz./ 907 g of canned diced tomatoes (*or fresh*)

6 oz. / 170 g. can tomato paste

7 small dates, pitted or 5 tsp. sugar (*only use dates if blending your sauce*)

½ medium yellow onion, diced

2 cloves of garlic

2 tsp. fresh basil, minced

1 tsp. dried oregano

Dash of salt (*to taste*)

¼-½ tsp. of black pepper

Directions:

1. Core the cabbage and gently place it into a large 5-6 qt. / L boiling pot of water. Slide in using a large mesh strainer to prevent splashing. Boil for a few minutes until you see the outer leaves loosen and the cabbage start to change color. Remove the cabbage from the pot, rinse it under cool water, and then let it cool completely before handling.

2. Place sauce ingredients into blender or food processor and blend until smooth. Pour into large saucepan and bring to a boil over medium heat. Reduce to low and simmer for 15-20 minutes stirring occasionally. Taste, and adjust with sugar, salt and pepper to your liking.

3. Bring large pot of water back to a boil. Pull cabbage leaves off gently being careful not to rip them. Cut away the core as necessary to remove leaves. Put 4-6 leaves at a time into boiling water and boil for 5 or 6 minutes until the stem softens and the color changes from bright green to yellowish green. Remove from pot with tongs, place in a colander, and rinse with cool water. Repeat with all of the leaves until you get to the small core. Drain leaves. Gently squeeze excess water from leaves before using.

* **If using canned beans and lentils, skip the following steps.**

To cook dried beans:

1. Soak white beans overnight.

2. Put in pressure cooker with 3 bay leaves and salt and fill with water an inch above beans.

3. Bring to a boil, reduce to medium, and cook for 5-6 minutes. Make sure the beans are fully cooked and can be mashed easily.

4. Turn off heat and let pressure release of own accord. Pour off water and save bay leaves.

5. Put beans into a large bowl or food processor to puree.

***Alternatively you can cook the beans on the stove until tender 1 to 1½ hours.**

To cook dried lentils:

1. Place into a strainer and pick out any pebbles or debris. Rinse for 30 seconds.

2. Put in pressure cooker with 3 bay leaves and salt, and fill with water an inch above lentils.

3. Bring to a boil, reduce to medium and cook for 6 minutes. Turn off heat and let pressure release of own accord. Pour off water and put lentils into the bowl with the beans.

4. In a food processor, or using a potato masher, puree/mash the beans until smooth.

5. Add in remaining ingredients and stir to combine. Stir in 3-4 Tbsp. of the tomato sauce to add some flavor and moisture to the beans.

*Alternatively you can cook the lentils on the stove until tender for 40-45 minutes.

Bringing It All Together:

1. Preheat oven to 350°F /177° C.

2. Line a 9 x 13 casserole pan with small inner cabbage leaves *(if you have extra)*

3. Thoroughly dry cabbage leaves and cut off bottom 1-2 inches of hard stem. If any of the leaves are hard to roll, shave part of the spine off the back side of the leaf.

4. Take a large cabbage leaf with the stem side facing towards you and spoon in 3-4 tablespoons of the filling at the bottom of the leaf. Roll the stem up and away from you and then fold in the sides and continue rolling. Keep the rolls tight to keep the filling in, but not so tight they are stretched as they may split.

5. Repeat with each roll.

6. Place rolls into casserole dish 3 across and 4 down.

7. Spoon the sauce over the rolls evenly. Top with remaining small cabbage leaves. Cover dish tightly with tin foil and bake for 1 hour and 15 minutes to 1 hour and 30 minutes (depending on how tender your beans and cabbage are)

8. Serve warm.

Nutrition Facts: 12 Servings, Amount Per Serving: Calories 142.3 Total Fat 0.7 g Saturated Fat 0.1 g Sodium 166.9 mg Total Carbohydrate 30.4 g Dietary Fiber 8.9 g Sugars 8.0 g Protein 6.9 g

California (Uramaki style) Sushi Roll

The California roll is something most people are familiar with in Japanese sushi, but it contains fake crab meat (in the form of Pollock) so it's not vegan. These rolls use vegetables and avocado instead for that creamy California roll feel.

Comfort Foods from Europe and Asia

Makes 4 Rolls

Ingredients for Sushi Rice: *(recipe at end of directions)*

2 cups white or brown sushi rice *(short grain)*

2 cups filtered water

3 Tbsp. rice vinegar

2 Tbsp. sugar

1 tsp. Herbamare or salt *(use more if desired, but sushi is dipped in salty soy sauce)*

Tools Needed for Rice:

Fine mesh strainer or sieve

Rice paddle or wooden spoon

Large Wooden/Glass/Ceramic/Plastic bowl *(NOT metal)*

Ingredients for Rolls:

4 pieces nori seaweed

8 sticks julienned cucumber *(see my post on prepping sushi veggies http://lowfatveganchef.*

com/how-to-prep-veggies-for-vegan-sushi/)

8 sticks julienned carrots, steamed gently

8-12 slices of avocado *(1 avocado)*

Directions:

For step-by-step photo instructions see my post at http://lowfatveganchef.com/how-to-make-a-vegan-california-sushi-roll-uramaki/

1. Measure between ¾ and 1 cup of sushi rice depending how much rice you want on your roll. *(Bear in mind that they're filling, usually a person can only eat 2 of these rolls.)* I used a heaping ¾ cup of rice and it was just right.

2. Lay your nori sheet SHINY side up *(dotted line side face down)*. This is the backside of your *nori* sheet and we're going to cover it with rice. Dump your rice into the middle of the *nori* sheet.

3. Using your rice paddles *(or very wet fingers)* gently push the rice outwards and to the edges and corners. This will take a while until you get the hang of it. You can leave a tiny space on the top and bottom of the sheet and this will make the roll easier to roll up. Continue spreading out the rice until you have a layer about 1-2 rice grains thick. It won't be perfect, but as long as there are no big gaps it's fine.

4. Press the rice down on your *nori* sheet so it's level, with no grains sticking up.

5. Pick up your *nori* sheet from the bottom, holding tightly, and flip it over away from you, with the rice side down. The dotted section side should be facing you.

6. Fill your *nori* sheet with the desired filling. For my vegan California roll, lay 2 strips of cucumber lengthwise, 2 strips of carrot and 2-3 slices of avocado. Spread them out so they fill the entire roll. It can spill out a little over the side, but not too much. Your filling should lie in the first rectangular area of the sheet, after the little bottom bar.

7. Grab the bottom of the sushi mat and bring it up and over creating a tube. Tuck and squeeze it between your hands and the sushi mat so you can't see the filling. Make each roll tight so your sushi stays together and the filling won't fall out the middle when you slice it. Roll your *nori* sheet up to the end. You shouldn't have to wet the end of the *nori* to seal it. It has moisture from the sticky rice. Squeeze it firmly and evenly all across the mat. When you get to the end, seal the roll evenly.

8. Flip your sushi roll over so the seam side is faced down. Get a very sharp knife, wet it thoroughly

with water and make a 6-8 cuts to the sushi roll to create sushi pieces. Bear in mind that this takes time and patience. You MUST wet your knife between EACH cut because your knife will be covered in sticky starch from the rice. If you don't you can tear and mangle your pretty sushi roll. I generally cut these ones into 6 pieces. But if you're feeding children, it'd be better at 8 pieces so it's not too big for them to bite into.

9. Plate your sushi and serve with soy sauce or tamari and chopsticks!

How to Make Perfect Sushi Rice

1. Measure out 2 cups dried sushi rice. This makes enough sushi for at least 4 large rolls and a small roll or two. It makes enough for 2 adults for dinner, or two single lunches.

2. Rinse rice through a fine metal sieve until water runs clear, OR soak in a large bowl of water and mix around by hand to get the excess starch off. Rinse and soak a few times until the water is clearer. This is important and will make your rice turn out better. Or you can let the rice soak for 30 minutes.

3. Place rice and 2 cups water into rice cooker or pot. (*If using more rice, always use a 1:1 ratio of rice to water*)

4a Rice cooker instructions: Set the white rice program and let it cook. When the rice is done and the buzzer goes off, leave the rice for 10 minutes to steam. Don't open it and don't touch it. (**see NOTE, below**)

4b Stovetop instructions: In a pot, place the rinsed rice and equal parts of water and bring to a boil. Stir the rice occasionally to prevent any grains from sticking to the bottom of the pot. Once it reaches a boil, turn the heat down to medium low, cover with a lid and steam. Do NOT open the lid until the rice is done steaming. You'll lose your moisture and heat and jeopardize the even cooking of your rice. Use a clear glass lid if you need to see. The rice is done when the water disappears—usually between 8 and 10 minutes depending on your stove. Remove the rice from heat.

5. Measure 3 Tbsp. of rice vinegar, 2 Tbsp. granulated sugar and 1 tsp. Herbamare or salt. Use more salt if you want, but it's really not necessary if you dip your sushi in soy sauce, which is salty.

6. Make sushi vinegar. Heat a small pot (not metal) over medium heat and add vinegar, sugar and Herbamare (or salt). Stir. When it's bubbling and everything is dissolved, remove from heat and let cool.

7. Remove rice from pot or rice cooker with a wooden spoon or a plastic rice scoop. Scrape the bottom and dump the sushi rice in 1 or 2 strokes so you don't end up mashing it. Pour into a wooden, glass, or plastic bowl. Do NOT put it into a metal mixing bowl. You risk ruining the flavor as vinegar reacts with metal. Scoop out only the rice that is perfectly cooked. If any is stuck or undercooked, leave it in the pot.

8. Gently cut the sushi rice with paddle to break it up.

9. Season the sushi rice by drizzling sushi vinegar evenly across it. Cut into the rice gently, again, to combine and spread out the seasoning. Now, let your rice cool. If it's too warm it can stick to the sushi mat and be hard to work with.

NOTE: My favorite rice cooker is the *Zojirushi* 5 1/2 cup rice cooker because it has settings for white rice, brown rice, mixed rice, porridge and cake. Yes, you can even cook *cake* in this rice cooker! If fancy rice cookers aren't your thing, check out the Hamilton Beach rice cooker. I use it when cooking at my mom's house. It has never overcooked or burned the rice. I used to use those $10 rice cookers with nothing by an on/off button, but often they'd turn off *before* the rice was done or overheat and cause overcooked or crusty rice. If cooking for a family, I highly suggest getting a decent rice cooker to free you up from the stove and the guesswork!

Nutritional Information: (contains 3 cups cooked rice) 2 Servings, Amount Per Serving: Calories 475.2 Total Fat 13.9 g Saturated Fat 1.9 g Sodium 735 mg Total Carbohydrate 81.1 g Dietary Fiber 9.1g Sugars 14.9 g Protein 9.5 g

Cauliflower Potato Frittata

You *rarely* find a vegan version of frittata. So, when you're *craving* this savory breakfast dish, *treat your taste buds* and make *this* one!

Makes 6 slices

Ingredients:

3 cups cauliflower florets cut into 1 inch pieces

1½ cups potatoes, peeled and cut into 1 inch cubes *(about 3 small potatoes)*

1 cup onion, diced *(1/2 large or 1 small one)*

1 12-14 oz. / 340-397 g package of medium firm tofu, drained

3 cloves of garlic, chopped

¾ tsp. turmeric powder

2-3 Tbsp. nutritional yeast

1 tsp. *Herbes de Provence*

¼ tsp. smoked paprika

½ tsp. *Herbamare* or salt

Dash of pepper

Cooking spray

Directions:

1. Preheat the oven to 425° F / 246° C.

2. Cut cauliflower into florets about 1 inch across, or smaller. If the cauliflower pieces are too large, they'll cause your frittata to fall apart.

3. Peel and slice onion from top to bottom and then slice the halves as thinly as possible.

4. Separate the onion, and add to cauliflower and cubed potatoes. Place on baking sheet and lightly spritz with cooking spray.

5. Roast the cauliflower, potato and onion for 30 minutes, stirring once or twice.

6. Turn the oven down to 375° F / 190° C *(on convection bake if available).*

7. In a food processor, combine the tofu, garlic, salt and remaining spices.

8. Transfer roasted vegetables to a skillet or pie pan. Spread out the tofu mixture on top of the vegetables and then gently work it down so that they are covered.

9. Bake the frittata for 40 minutes or until the top is starting to brown.

10. Let stand 10-15 minutes before serving to make slicing easier.

11. Cut into 6 slices. Serve & *enjoy!*

Nutrition Facts: 3 Servings, Amount Per Serving: Calories 289.9 Total Fat 10.5 g Saturated Fat 1.6 g Sodium 274.4 mg Total Carbohydrate 47.4 g Dietary Fiber 11.9 g Sugars 3.1 g Protein 26.4 g

Deluxe Spinach Mushroom Lasagna

Good vegan lasagna *isn't* something you often find at a restaurant. *This* one, however, is *delicious*, healthy and *flavorful - well worth the work!* This will impress even the most *skeptical* omnivore!

Serves 8 (if using a large 4.5 Qt./4.3 L lasagna pan)

For a smaller lasagna recipe in a smaller pan see variations at the end.

Ingredients:

One 1 lb./454 g package lasagna noodles *(16 noodles are needed)*

NOTE: For Gluten free, use Tinkyada brown rice lasagna noodles

Ingredients for Sauce:

1 large onion, diced

8-10 cloves garlic, minced

3 28 oz. / 794 g. cans fire roasted, whole or diced tomatoes

1/3 cup / 79 ml. tomato paste

½ cup fresh basil chopped

2 Tbsp. fresh oregano, packed

2 Tbsp. sugar or maple syrup

¾ -1 tsp. Herbamare or salt *(or to taste)*

½ tsp. pepper

Ingredients for Tofu Ricotta:

3 12.3 oz. / 349 g. packages silken tofu, firm *(2.3 lbs. total)*

8 cloves of garlic, minced

1/3 cup chopped basil

1 cup nutritional yeast

4 Tbsp. miso paste *(Genmai brown rice)*

2 Tbsp. fresh lemon juice

½ Tbsp. maple syrup or liquid sweetener

Ingredients for Mushroom Layer:

6 cups mushrooms, sliced

2 Tbsp. light soy sauce *(or gluten free light tamari)*

2 Tbsp. maple syrup or brown sugar

6 cloves garlic, minced

1 Tbsp. water

Ingredients for Spinach Layer:

2   10 oz. / 284 g. packages of frozen spinach, thawed

Ingredients for Topping

½ cup nutritional yeast

Fresh basil, chopped

NOTE: To save time, try making the sauce and tofu ricotta the day before.

Directions - Lasagna:

1. Using 2 wide medium depth pots *(or one very large pot)* bring water to a boil and then add salt if desired. Add lasagna noodles when at a rolling boil and cook for about 9 minutes. Stir occasionally to prevent noodles from sticking to bottom of pot. Drain and rinse to remove excess salt if desired. When slightly cool, carefully lay them out on parchment or wax paper individually so they do not stick together.

2. While the pasta water is boiling you can start on the sauce. In a large non-stick pan sauté the onions dry over medium heat for 6-7 minutes until translucent. Add the minced garlic. Stir occasionally so it doesn't burn. You can add a little vegetable broth or water if necessary to prevent sticking. Add the canned tomatoes and seasonings. Taste test and adjust if desired. Pour mixture into a Vitamix or blender. You may have to do two batches. Blend until smooth and then return to the pan to keep warm.

3. Preheat the oven to 400° F / 204° C. Drain the silken tofu and crumble into a large bowl. Add the seasonings and mix until combined. Ensure the miso is distributed evenly.

4. If doing the mushroom layer, sauté the mushrooms and seasonings in a non-stick pan over medium heat for 15 minutes, stirring occasionally. The mushrooms should release enough water that it doesn't stick. If you need a little extra water, you can add some. To cook faster, cover with a pot lid to steam.

5. Drain the spinach and gently squeeze out some of the water. You want a lot of it out, but not so that it is completely dry. This adds moisture to the lasagna.

6. When everything is ready, assemble the lasagna.

ASSEMBLY:

- In a large 4.5 qt. / 4.3 L. *(9"x13")* lasagna pan pour about 1 cup of sauce into the bottom and smooth it out.

- Lay 4 strips of lasagna gently overlapping each other. Add a third of the tofu and spread it out to roughly cover the lasagna noodles.

- Next add all of the spinach and spread it out as evenly as you can over the tofu.

- Pour 1½ cups of sauce over the spinach layer.

- Start the next layer of lasagna with 4 more lasagna noodles gently overlapping.

- Add another third of the tofu and spread it out.

- Next, layer the cooked mushrooms *(if you have them)* over the tofu.

- Pour another 1½ cups of sauce over the mushrooms.

- Layer 4 more lasagna noodles overlapping.

- Top with the remaining tofu.

- Pour 1½ cups of sauce over it.

- Top with 4 more lasagna noodles and pour the remaining sauce all over it.

- Garnish with chopped basil or nutritional yeast if desired.

7. Cover the pan tightly with tinfoil and bake for 30-60 minutes, depending on how thick you pan is. You want the middle of the lasagna to get hot. It cooks faster if you've kept your sauce and mushrooms warm. If you have a very thick ceramic pan like *Le Creuset,* you may have to cook it 1 hour to 1 hour and 15 minutes. Glass or thin metal pans will heat through much faster and can be checked at 30-40 minutes for doneness.

8. When lasagna is done, remove from oven and let stand 10 minutes for the sauce to settle and thicken. This is important so you can remove your lasagna in nice square slices. Slice with a sharp knife when slightly cool and serve immediately.

9. Enjoy with a side or Caesar salad, or garlic bread.

Additional Tips:

If you are prepping some of the ingredients the night before, like sauce, ricotta, or mushrooms, let them come to room temperature. The sauce is best heated on the stove before assembling the lasagna so that it takes less time to heat through.

Fresh herbs really make a difference in this recipe, but if you don't have them, you can use dried basil and oregano.

Slice and refrigerate or freeze any leftovers for an easy lunch or dinner.

Variations:

For smaller lasagna pans you're only going to use 12-15 noodles and do 3 layers instead of 4. **Reduce the amount of tofu ricotta:** silken tofu to 2 packages, 4 cloves of garlic, ¼ cup basil, 2/3 cup nutritional yeast, 2.5 tbsp miso, 1.5 tbsp lemon juice and 1 tsp. maple syrup. **Reduce the amount of pasta sauce:** 1 medium onion, 4-5 cloves of garlic, 2 28 oz. cans diced tomatoes, ¼ cup tomato paste, 1/3 cup fresh basil, 1 ½ tbsp. fresh oregano, 11/2 tbsp. sugar, ½ - ¾ tsp. Herbamare and 1/3 tsp. ground pepper.

You can add any vegetables you like to your lasagna. Just sauté or roast and season them beforehand, and use them in a layer on top of the tofu. Make sure they're tender enough before adding. Zucchini, eggplant, roasted red peppers; etc. would work well replacing the mushrooms in this recipe.

Nutrition Facts: 8 Servings Amount Per Serving Calories 451.9 Total Fat 15.4 g Saturated Fat 2.2 g Sodium 941.5 mg Total Carbohydrate 79.9 g Dietary Fiber 15.4 g Sugars 11.5 g Protein 44.5

Fettuccine Alfredo with Mushrooms & Spinach

This Alfredo sauce is so good you can fool *any* omnivore with it! A *delicious* low fat alternative to your old favorite creamy white sauce!

Serves 4

Ingredients:

1 lb. /454 g. of fettuccine or pasta of choice *(use Tinkyada for gluten free if desired)*

Ingredients for Mushrooms & Spinach:

1 lb. / 454 g. cleaned & trimmed gourmet mushrooms *(hedgehog, chanterelle, oyster, etc.)*

Pinch of salt

1 clove of garlic, minced

¼ tsp. Herbamare or salt

½ cup water

1 Tbsp. fresh thyme *(or 1 tsp. dried)*

6-8 cups fresh spinach *(or other greens of choice)*

2 Tbsp. white wine or cooking wine *There is wine in sauce as well*

Ingredients for Sauce:

1 medium sweet or regular onions, diced

2 Tbsp. white wine or cooking wine *There is wine in mushrooms & spinach as well*

12 oz. / 340 g. pkg. silken firm tofu *(mori-nu)*

1½ cups / 355.5 ml. almond milk, unsweetened original

1 small bulb of garlic

4-5 tsp. miso *(Genmai brown rice)* or 1–1-1/2 tsp. salt

½ tsp. fresh ground pepper

2 Tbsp. nutritional yeast

2-3 tsp. lemon juice

1 Tbsp. cornstarch

Directions:

1. Preheat oven to 450° F / 232° C. Clean and trim mushrooms. Fill a large pot with water and bring to a boil. Add salt if desired.

2. Cut top off of head of garlic for sauce and wrap in tinfoil. When the oven is heated, roast the garlic for about 30 minutes until soft. Unwrap when cool, being careful not to burn yourself. Set aside.

3. In a non-stick skillet, sauté onion for sauce over medium heat in 2 Tbsp. / 15 ml. white wine for 5-6 minutes. Stir continuously, careful not to burn. Set aside.

4. Add remaining ingredients for sauce into blender, aside from cornstarch. Squeeze in the roasted garlic, when cool. Blend until smooth. Taste test and adjust seasonings if desired. Add cornstarch and blend on low for a few seconds just to combine. Pour into a saucepan to reheat. Start heating your Alfredo sauce over medium heat while you cook the mushrooms. Stir often, scraping the bottom of the bottom to prevent burning. When heated through, remove from heat and cover with a lid.

5. Add pasta to pot of boiling. Remember to keep stirring your pasta while it cooks to prevent sticking and ensure even cooking. Stir frequently. When pasta is cooking, start the mushrooms. In a large non-stick skillet add the mushrooms, the seasonings, and 2 Tbsp. / 15 ml. wine and cook over medium heat for 10 minutes uncovered. Stir often. Add spinach when pasta is almost done cooking and cook for another 2-3 minutes until wilted.

6. When pasta is done to desired tenderness, drain. Pour pasta into hot pasta sauce and toss to coat. You can add the sautéed mushrooms and onions into the mix, or use as a garnish.

7. Serve.

Additional Tips:

You can use this sauce with any kind of pasta.

Omit the mushrooms and spinach for a quicker dish or switch them out for other veggies.

Nutrition Facts: 4 Servings, Amount Per Serving: Calories 403.6 Total Fat 5.4 g Saturated Fat 0.6 g Sodium 560.2 mg Total Carbohydrate 61.0 g Dietary Fiber 7.8 g Sugars 2.9 g Protein 21.0 g

Gourmet Chanterelle Mushroom and Spinach Risotto

I absolutely *adore* mushroom risotto, but it's something I only eat at home as it's difficult to get a *vegan version* at a restaurant. My risotto skips the oil and fat and is *still* creamy and flavorful. For best results I suggest making your own vegetable broth or even a mushroom broth. You will be *greatly rewarded* if you *do!*

Comfort Foods from Europe and Asia

Serves 2 entree or 4 side servings

Risotto Ingredients:

6-7 cups / 1.4—1.65 L. vegetable broth *(homemade low sodium is best)*

1½ cups Arborio rice

1 large onion, chopped finely

3-4 cloves of garlic, minced

¾ cup / 177 mL white wine

1 tsp. dried thyme

1 tsp. parsley

2 bay leaves

1-2 handfuls of baby spinach *(or other greens)*

3 Tbsp. nutritional yeast

Salt to taste

Fresh ground pepper to taste

Sautéed Mushrooms Ingredients:

1 lb. / 454 g package of Chanterelle, hedgehog or other gourmet mushrooms, cleaned and sliced

½ cup / 118 ml. vegetable broth

2 Tbsp. white wine

½ tsp. maple syrup or liquid sweetener

Salt to taste

Fresh ground pepper to taste

Directions:

1. Add 1/2 cup vegetable broth to a large pan over medium-high heat. When hot, add onion, garlic, salt, and pepper. Reduce heat to medium and stir frequently until onion is very soft and browned, 15-20 minutes. If onion starts to scorch, reduce heat further and stir in 2 Tbsp. water.

2. Meanwhile cook chanterelle mushrooms in ½ cup of vegetable broth with 2 Tbsp. of white wine, ½ tsp. of maple syrup. Sauté mushrooms until tender. Season to taste with salt and pepper. Set aside.

3. Add rice to onions and stir until opaque, about 3 minutes. Add white wine and stir over medium heat until absorbed, 1 to 2 minutes. Add 6 cups broth one cup at a time and dried herbs, stirring after each addition of broth until almost absorbed, 20 to 25 minutes total *(rice should be just tender to bite)*. Stir in baby spinach until wilted. Remove from heat and stir in nutritional yeast.

4. Serve.

Nutrition Facts: 4 Servings, Amount Per Serving: Calories 168.5 Total Fat 0.9 g Saturated Fat 0.1 g Sodium 282.8 mg Total Carbohydrate 27.0 g Dietary Fiber 6.7 g Sugars 3.4 g Protein 7.3 g

Greek Rice Stuffed Peppers

When I traveled in Greece I sampled several vegan versions of stuffed vegetables. Greek rice stuffed peppers was one of my favorites. I switched out the traditional *Arborio* rice for brown rice to make this *a whole grain version.* If you like the combination of lemon and dill you're going to *love* these! When I serve these at dinner parties *they're a huge hit!*

Serves 3-4 for entrées or 6-8 as a side dish

Ingredients:

6 large or 8 small bell peppers *(any color but green)*

1 large onion, diced

3 medium carrots, peeled and diced

3 small zucchinis, peeled and diced

1 cup / 236 ml. vegetable broth

3 cups cooked brown rice

5 Tbsp. tomato paste

¾ cup fresh parsley, chopped

¾ cup fresh dill, chopped

½ -1 lemon, juiced

¼ tsp. fresh ground pepper

¾ tsp. Herbamare or salt

1 lemon—cut into wedges *(optional)*

Directions:

1. Preheat oven to 350°F /175° C. Cut tops off of peppers like you would a jack-o-lantern, remove seeds, and wash thoroughly.

2. Place in an oven safe dish arranged upright and put tops back on. Bake at for 30 minutes.

3. Meanwhile in a large pan sauté onions, carrots and zucchini in vegetable broth for 5-6 minutes.

4. Stir in the rice and tomato paste and coat thoroughly.

5. Add parsley, dill, lemon juice, pepper, and *Herbamare* and stir to combine.

6. When peppers are ready, remove from oven and fill with stuffing.

7. Place tops back on peppers and bake for an extra 30-40 minutes until peppers are soft.

8. Serve additional wedges of lemon if desired.

Additional Tips:

Don't use green peppers. Green peppers are unripe and much harder. They will not be done in time if you cook them along with red, yellow or orange peppers.

You can substitute white rice if you like.

Nutrition Facts: 6 Servings, Amount Per Serving: Calories 170.9 Total Fat 1.4 g Saturated Fat 0.3 g Sodium 325.7 mg Total Carbohydrate 37.1 g Dietary Fiber 5.6 g Sugars 3.6 g Protein 4.4 g

Indian Cauliflower Potato Curry (Aloo Gobi)

This is a *delicious* and *mildly spiced* curry, excellent for those skeptical about eating Indian food. Cauliflower and potatoes *go so well together* it was like *they were meant to be!*

Comfort Foods from Europe and Asia

Serves 6

Ingredients:

4 large waxy potatoes

2/3 head of cauliflower

1 small onion, or ½ large, diced

1 cup / 118 ml vegetable broth

4 cloves of garlic minced

2 tsp. ginger minced

1 ½ tsp. roasted cumin

1 tsp. ground coriander

¼ tsp. turmeric

¼ - ½ tsp. cayenne or chipotle chili powder

¼ -½ tsp. *garam masala*

½ - 1 tsp. salt

fresh ground pepper

fresh cilantro to garnish

Directions:

1. In a large deep skillet sauté the onions, ginger and garlic in 1 cup vegetable broth for 5-6 minutes. Add the potatoes and spices except for garam masala and salt and turn heat to medium-high. Cover with a lid and cook the potatoes until you can just pierce with a fork. They will still be undercooked.

2. Add the cauliflower. Make sure there is still enough liquid in the pan. If not add a little bit more just enough to steam. Bring heat to medium and cook until cauliflower and potatoes are just tender. Make sure to not overcook the vegetables.

3. Add *Herbamare, garam masala,* fresh pepper and coriander and stir gently to mix. When stirring be very gentle to not break up the potatoes too much. Use a large spatula. Your vegetables should be dry and no water remaining.

4. Serve with basmati rice or roti bread, and *enjoy!*

Nutrition Facts: 6 Servings, Amount Per Serving: Calories 227.3 Total Fat 0.6 g Saturated Fat 0.1 g Sodium 262.4 mg Total Carbohydrate 50.8 g Dietary Fiber 8.4 g Sugars 2.3 g Protein 7.3 g

Taj Mahal in Agra. Photo: Wikimedia Commons

Indian Chickpea Curry (Chana Masala)

This is often *everyone's* favorite curry! I make mine a little different—it's *less spicy* and *more savory* with a variety of spices. Serve this with rice for a *quick meal!*

Serves 4

Ingredients:

1 large onion, diced

1 ½ Tbsp. ginger minced

5 cloves garlic minced

2 14.5 oz. / 411 g. can of fire roasted tomatoes

2 15 oz. / 425 g. cans of chickpeas, drained (about 3 1/2 -4 cups cooked)

1 ½ - 2 ½ tsp. sugar *optional

4 tsp. roasted ground cumin

1 Tbsp. coriander powder

½ tsp. turmeric

¼ tsp. cardamom

¼ tsp. cinnamon

¼ -½ tsp. cayenne or chipotle chili pepper

¾ - 1 tsp. *Herbamare* or salt

½ lime, juiced

Fresh black pepper

1 handful of cilantro, chopped (to garnish)

1 cup / 237 ml. vegetable broth or water as needed

Directions:

1. Sauté the onions, ginger and garlic dry in a non-stick pan over medium heat for 8-10 minutes. Add vegetable broth or water as needed to prevent sticking.

2. Add the tomatoes and spices except for salt and pepper and sauté for another 10 minutes until tomatoes are broken down and soft.

3. Add chickpeas and turn heat down to low and cook for 15-20 minutes until chickpeas are tender.

4. Add the *Herbamare*, lime and black pepper and taste test. Add more heat if desired.

5. Transfer into serving dish and garnish with chopped cilantro if desired.

6. Serve with basmati rice or Indian flat bread such as roti.

Nutrition Facts: 4 Servings, Amount Per Serving: Calories 222.4 Total Fat 3.3 g Saturated Fat 0.0 g Sodium 662.5 mg Total Carbohydrate 42.5 g Dietary Fiber 11.5 g Sugars 11.8 g Protein 10.6 g

Indian Eggplant Curry (Bhaingan Bharta)

This is hands down my *favorite* Indian curry! I like to serve this along with my *chana masala* and basmati rice for a *delicious* Indian feast for my friends and family!

Serves 4

Ingredients:

2 large eggplants	1 tsp. roasted ground cumin
1 large onion, diced	½ tsp. turmeric
1 red pepper, seeded and cut into chunks	1 ¼ tsp. ground coriander
1 14.5 oz. / 411 g. can fire roasted tomatoes	¼ - ½ tsp. cayenne or chipotle chili powder
1 cup vegetable broth	½ -3/4 tsp. *Herbamare* or salt
4 tsp. ginger, minced	1/8 -¼ tsp. *garam masala*
4 cloves of garlic, minced	1 handful of cilantro, chopped *(for garnish)*

Directions:

1. Pierce eggplants with a fork all over and roast at 400°F / 204°C for 45-50 minutes until completely soft in center and skin is blackened a bit. Alternatively, you can roast them over an open flame on low until the skin is blackened and they shrivel and are soft in the middle.

2. Let the eggplant cool before handling. Peel or scoop out the inside flesh and chop into chunks. Set aside.

3. Sauté the onions and garlic in vegetable broth for 8-10 minutes. Add the bell pepper and ginger and sauté for another minute. Add spices except for salt and *garam masala* and the tomatoes. Cook for 5 minutes to break down. Add the eggplant and cook for another 10-20 minutes depending how soft it is. Keep stirring to prevent sticking. Once creamy and all the seeds are soft add the salt and *garam masala*. Stir to combine and taste test. Add more heat if desired.

4. Transfer to serving dish and garnish with chopped cilantro.

5. Serve with basmati rice or Indian flatbread such as roti, and *enjoy!*

Additional Tips:

Eggplant is very forgiving and can be cooked quite a long time. Keep it on low heat on the stove if you're cooking more than 1 dish at a time. Just stir occasionally to prevent anything from sticking while it keeps warm.

Nutrition Facts: 4 Servings, Amount Per Serving: Calories 129.8 Total Fat 0.6 g Saturated Fat 0.1 g. Sodium 265.7 mg Total Carbohydrate 30.2 g Dietary Fiber 10.7 g Sugars 4.5 g Protein 4.8 g

Indian Spiced Basmati Rice with Peas

This is a simple spiced rice recipe you *can serve with your favorite Indian curry*. You can even turn this into *a main dish on its own*, by adding more of your favorite vegetables, turmeric or curry powder, and raisins for a quick *biryani!*

Serves 6 (Yields 6 cups cooked rice)

Ingredients:

2 cups white basmati rice

Water *(see directions)*

1 medium onion, minced

1 cup of frozen peas *optional*

1 tsp. *Herbamare* or salt

1 small cinnamon stick

3 green cardamom pods

3 whole cloves

2 tsp. cumin seeds

Stove Top Instructions:

1. Soak rice in enough water to cover for 20 minutes.

2. Mince onion. Heat a non-stick skillet over medium low heat and toast the spices for a minute or two, being careful not to burn them. Then add the onion and sauté for about 10 minutes.

3. Drain the rice and add to the pan and sauté for 2-3 minutes.

4. Transfer everything to a pot; add 3 cups of water, peas and *Herbamare* or salt. Bring to a boil and then cover and reduce to low. You are essentially steaming the rice. Do not lift the lid until done! Cook 18-20 minutes or until all water is absorbed.

5. Remove from heat and let stand 5 minutes to finish steaming.

6. Fluff with a fork and serve.

Rice Cooker Instructions:

1. Use scoop with your rice cooker to measure 2 cups of rice. Soak rice in enough cold water to cover for 15 minutes.

2. Mince onion. Heat a non-stick skillet and toast the spices for a minute or two, careful not to burn them. Then add the onion and sauté for about 10 minutes.

3. Drain the rice; add to the pan and sauté for 2-3 minutes.

4. Transfer everything to the rice cooker and add about 3 - 3¼ cups *(the cup that came with the rice cooker)*, and peas and *Herbamare* or salt.

5. Turn rice cooker on to white rice setting and cook.

6. When finished let stand 10 minutes to finish steaming and then fluff with a fork and serve.

Additional Tips:

Whole spices are best to use. Indian rice is delicate and you don't want to over season it with ground spices in the wrong ratio.

If you only need a few whole spices, check out a health food store or Indian market, find the bulk section, and get enough to make a few recipes. Then you can decide if you like the flavor of these whole spices before investing in a larger quantity.

Or, buy whole spices online along with a simple coffee grinder and *grind your own* fresh spices. They'll be more *fragrant* and *flavorful!*

Variation:

If you don't like peas, omit them from the recipe and switch to frozen carrot cubes if desired.

Nutrition Facts: 6 Servings, Amount Per Serving: Calories 200.4 Total Fat 0.1 g Saturated Fat 0.0 g Sodium 254.1 mg Total Carbohydrate 45.7 g Dietary Fiber 1.3 g Sugars 1.3 g Protein 5.0 g

Indian Spinach Potato Curry (Aloo Palak)

This curry is a *great* alternative to *Palak Paneer (Indian cheese and spinach curry)!* You still get the flavor of the *pureed* savory spinach, and the potatoes fill it out *more* to create a hearty main dish!

Comfort Foods from Europe and Asia

Serves 4

Ingredients:

1 lb. / 454 g. fresh spinach

2 inches of ginger, minced

4 medium onions, diced

2 green chilies, minced *optional

6 garlic cloves, minced

2 large potatoes

1 tsp. turmeric powder

1 tsp. salt

2 tsp. cumin seeds

1 tsp. roasted cumin

1 tsp. roasted coriander

2 tsp. *garam masala*

2-3 Tbsp. unsweetened almond or coconut milk *optional

Directions:

1. In a pan, cook the spinach with garlic, ginger, onions and the green chilies for about 5-10 minutes.
2. Remove from pan, blend to a fine puree, and put aside.
3. Boil the potatoes with salt and turmeric for 10 minutes and set aside.
4. Add cumin seeds along with spinach-onion paste back into the pan and simmer for a few minutes.
5. Add the cooked potatoes, *garam masala*, coriander and cumin powder and a little water if needed. Add almond milk for a creamier texture.
6. Simmer for a few minutes until the potatoes absorb the flavor.
7. Serve and enjoy!

Nutrition Facts: 4 Servings, Amount Per Serving: Calories 160.8 Total Fat 0.9 g Saturated Fat 0.1 g Sodium 697.5 mg Total Carbohydrate 36.1 g Dietary Fiber 7.0 g Sugars 2.9 g Protein 7.9 g

Photo: Bernard Gagnon. Wikimedia Commons.

Moroccan Root Vegetable Tajine

Tajine is a North African dish named for the special clay pot with a cone-shaped lid it's usually cooked in. You can make a *tajine* at home with any casserole baking dish and an oven. *Chermoula* is a spicy marinade or rub that is used in Moroccan, Algerian and Tunisian cooking to flavor meat and vegetables.

Comfort Foods from Europe and Asia

Serves 6

Ingredients for *Tajine:*

1 lb. / 454 g. parsnips, chopped *(4 medium)*

1 large yam/sweet potato, chopped

1 red onion, chopped

1 lb. / 454 g. carrots, chopped *(4 medium-large)*

4 cups cooked chickpeas, or 2 15 oz./ 425 g. cans

16 dried apricots cut into thirds *(look for sulfur free)*

2 cups / 473 ml. of water or low sodium vegetable broth

Ingredients for *Chermoula* paste:

2 medium red onions cut into chunks

6 garlic cloves

2 tsp. ginger, minced

2½ Tbsp. lemon juice *(1 lemon)*

1 Tbsp. roasted cumin

1 Tbsp. smoked paprika

1 tsp. cinnamon

1 tsp. roasted coriander

1 tsp. turmeric powder

½ -1 tsp. chili powder *optional

1-2 Tbsp. honey or agave (or chopped pitted dates)

½ cup fresh cilantro, chopped (1/2 bunch)

1½ tsp. Herbamare or salt

Directions:

1. Preheat oven to 350°F /175° C.

2. Using 2 large non-stick skillets, sauté *tajine* ingredients *(except chickpeas and apricots)* over medium high heat for 10 min. Remove from heat and transfer to a very large mixing bowl.

3. Using a Vitamix or food processor, combine the chermoula ingredients until smooth. Add sweetness or chili depending on your preference. Use the plunger if you have a *Vitamix,* or blend in 2 batches if you have a small food processor. If you taste the sauce it will probably taste overwhelmingly spicy from the raw onion. Don't panic. Once cooked, it mellows significantly and tastes like a slightly sweetened savory stew.

4. Pour the chermoula paste over the vegetables in a large mixing bowl. Stir to combine and then add the chickpeas and apricots. Stir until evenly coated.

5. Pour the stew into a large lasagna size casserole dish. Spread out the vegetables evenly and cover with 2 cups of water. Cover with tinfoil tightly.

6. Bake in a preheated oven for 1 hour 45 min to 2 h 10 min or until the sweet potato is tender and cooked through. Once cooked, stir to redistribute the sauce throughout the liquid.

7. Serve over couscous or quinoa with wedges of lemon.

Additional Tips:

Peel and chop vegetables into chunks about an inch to inch and half thick. To keep the chopped onion mostly intact, cut off the top, slice in half evenly through the root, and peel. Shave the root hairs off of the base of the onion so the bottom end holds together. Then slice into wedges.

If you're short on time, cut your veggies into smaller ½ inch chunks so they'll cook faster. Adjust cooking time and check veggies after 1 h 15 minutes.

Don't worry if the *chermoula* paste tastes very spicy and bitter when raw. Once it's cooked and mixed with the water and vegetable cooking juices it becomes milder and tastes much better!

Nutrition Facts: 6 Servings, Amount Per Serving: Calories 449.1 Total Fat 3.0 g Saturated Fat 0.4 g Sodium 868.8 mg Total Carbohydrate 98.5 g Dietary Fiber 17.7 g Sugars 20.6 g Protein 12.5 g

Ratatouille

I *love* this Ratatouille! I have made it many times, and I prefer this method. It's similar to Julia Child's cooking method—but of course *without* any oil!

Comfort Foods from Europe and Asia

Serves 4

Ingredients:

1 eggplant

1 zucchini

1 onion - chopped

1 cup / 237 ml. vegetable broth

2 15 oz. /425 g cans / 4 cups of diced tomatoes, Italian flavor

1 Tbsp. *Herbs de Provence*

2 cups carrots cut into matchsticks

1 cup red pepper, cut into chunks *(1 pepper)*

Salt to taste

Fresh ground pepper to taste

Directions:

1. Peel eggplant, cut into quarters, salt and drain for 30 minutes. (The salt sweats the eggplant and draws the bitter flavor out of it)

2. Cut zucchini into halves

3. Sauté onion in vegetable broth and add tomatoes. Season it with Herbs de Provence, salt, and pepper.

4. Add carrots to tomato sauce and cook on medium low.

5. Sauté eggplant, zucchini and peppers separately. Then add to tomato sauce and heat through.

Nutrition Facts: 4 Servings, Amount Per Serving: Calories 126.6 Total Fat 0.8 g Saturated Fat 0.1 g Sodium 53.1 mg Total Carbohydrate 29.5 g Dietary Fiber 8.8 g Sugars 2.9 g Protein 5.0 g

Rotini with Chanterelle Mushrooms in a Red Wine Tomato Sauce

This is a simple yet rustic Italian dish that once you taste, you'll *swear* it was produced in Italy! If you *ever* have a little red wine left over, save it to use for *this incredible dish!*

Serves 4

Ingredients:

12.3 oz. / 350 g of rotini pasta *(gluten free if desired)*

3 cups chanterelle mushrooms, cleaned

3 cups cherry tomatoes halved or Roma tomatoes, diced

1 cup / 237 ml. vegetable broth or bouillon in water

½ large sweet onion, chopped

2-3 garlic cloves, minced

2/3 - ¾ cup / 118-177 ml red wine *(use drinking wine, not a salty cooking wine)*

3 Tbsp. tomato paste

1 tsp. sugar

½ tsp. *Herbamare* or salt

¼ - ½ tsp. fresh pepper

1 bunch of parsley, minced

NOTE: If using a *whole* bag of pasta *(1 lb./454g)* double the sauce recipe. If your pasta *is gluten free* or whole grain you may want to double the sauce recipe as well, as they can be a little bland. It also depends on how saucy you like your marinara!

Directions:

1. Bring a large 5-6 qt. / L. pot of water to a rolling boil and add salt if desired. Add the pasta and cook until al dente, about 9 minutes. Remove the pasta when cooked and set aside.

2. Meanwhile, sauté the onions and garlic in vegetable broth for 3-4 minutes. Add the mushrooms and cook for another minute or two.

3. Add the tomatoes and cook for 5 more minutes. You should have enough broth and juices to cook with, if not add a little more broth or water. Add the red wine and tomato paste and cook over medium heat for 25 minutes until the liquid evaporates a little and the tomatoes cook down.

4. Season with salt, pepper and sugar. Taste and adjust seasonings as desired.

5. Add the cooked rotini noodles and toss in the sauce for 3 to 4 minutes until it's reheated and cooked to desired tenderness. Add the minced parsley and toss.

6. Serve and enjoy!

Nutrition Facts: 4 Servings, Amount Per Serving: Calories 364.3 Total Fat 1.9 g Saturated Fat 0.0 g Sodium 311.2 mg Total Carbohydrate 76.9 g Dietary Fiber 12.2 g Sugars 7.5 g Protein 12.7 g

Spaghetti Marinara with French Lentils

This is a classic favorite with a *healthy twist!* French lentils are a *great substitute* for ground beef, and make this a very *hearty* and *satisfying* dish!

Serves 2

Ingredients for Sauce:

4 cups peeled, deseeded tomatoes *(or 32 oz. / 907 g canned tomatoes)*

4-5 small dates *(or 2-3 large medjool dates)* pitted

1/8 cup fresh basil leaves

1 Tbsp. *Herbs de Provence (or Italian herb mix)*

½ cup onion, minced

2-3 cloves of garlic, minced

½ tsp. *Herbamare* or salt

½ cup French green or brown lentils, soaked

1 cup / 237 ml. vegetable stock or water *(to cook with)*

PLUS: 6 oz. / 170 grams of spaghetti *(gluten free if desired)*

NOTE: To peel tomatoes, immerse in boiling water for 1 minute and immediately place in an ice water bath. Peel and cut into halves or quarters and de-seed.

Directions:

1. Place tomatoes, dates, basil and *Herbs de Provence* into a *Vitamix* or blender and blend until smooth.

2. In a pot, add a little water or vegetable stock and place on medium high heat. Once heated, add the onions and sauté until translucent. Add water or stock as necessary. Add the garlic and sauté 1 minute longer.

3. Drain soaked lentils. Add tomato sauce to pot, season with *Herbamare* and add lentils.

4. Cook sauce over medium heat for 30-40 minutes until lentils are at desired tenderness.

*Alternately you can cook the lentils in a pressure cooker for 10 minutes and add to sauce to reduce cooking time for tender lentils.

5. Meanwhile, bring a large 4-6 qt./3.7-5.7 L. pot of water to a boil. Taste sauce, adding a little more salt or pepper if desired.

6. Cook pasta according to package directions, about 9-10 minutes.

7. Toss pasta with sauce in bowls and serve. Garnish with fresh basil if desired.

8. Serve and *enjoy!*

Nutrition Facts: 2 Servings, Amount Per Serving: Calories 457.5 Total Fat 1.5 g Saturated Fat 0.0 g Sodium 765.5 mg Total Carbohydrate 100.3 g Dietary Fiber 19.3 g Sugars 14.3 g Protein 23 g

Thai Basil and Chili Eggplant Stir Fry With Broccoli

This is my *favorite* stir-fry! I love having eggplant and broccoli together, and the chili and Thai basil give a *new* spin to an old staple. Make sure you choose the long skinny Japanese style eggplant for this recipe. It's much milder and less bitter than regular eggplant.

Comfort Foods from Europe and Asia

Serves 2

Ingredients for Chile Sauce:

3 Tbsp. low sodium soy sauce (or gluten-free tamari)

2 Tbsp. brown sugar

½ tsp. rice vinegar or white vinegar

½ fresh or dried Thai chili, minced

1 tsp. cornstarch mixed with 1 tbsp. water

3 cloves of garlic, minced

1 Tbsp. ginger, minced

Ingredients for Stir Fry:

1 cup / 237 ml. vegetable broth (low sodium or homemade) or low sodium bouillon in water

1 long Japanese eggplant (light purple in color)

2 cups mushrooms, sliced

1 small onion cut into large chunks

1 crown of broccoli cut into large florets

1 bunch of Thai basil - stems removed and torn

* Serve with Jasmine or Brown Rice, follow basic rice instructions.

Directions:

1. Combine the soy sauce, brown sugar, vinegar and chili in a small bowl. Set aside. Combine the cornstarch with water and set aside.

2. Heat a non-stick pan over medium high heat. When hot, add the broth, half of the garlic, all of the ginger and mushrooms and sauté for 2 minutes.

3. Add the eggplant and 1 Tbsp. of sauce and then cover the pot with a lid and cook for 4-5 minutes.

4. Add the remaining sauce and the onions and broccoli and cover and cook for 2-3 minutes. If it needs a little more liquid add another Tbsp. or two of water or broth.

5. When the eggplant is soft add the rest of the garlic and the cornstarch mixture and stir-fry another minute. The sauce will thicken. Remove from heat and stir in the Thai basil to wilt.

6. Serve with jasmine or brown rice.

Additional Tips:

I find it spicy enough to use only half of a Thai chili pepper. If you like it *really* spicy you can add a whole one. Be very careful not to touch your face or eyes after chopping it, and wash your hands well.

Use the lowest sodium soy sauce you can find. Additionally you can dilute it a bit and make it lower in sodium as well.

Add the mushrooms first as they take a bit longer to cook. If you'd like to substitute other vegetables, like bell peppers *(capsicum)* you can add them with the broccoli. Add other vegetables like zucchini with the eggplant if you like them soft, or with the broccoli if you like them *al dente.*

If you don't like eggplant, use another stir fry vegetable. Most people just don't like *undercooked,* 'spongy' eggplant. Once cooked, it becomes soft and creamy. If seasoned well people enjoy it, much to their surprise!

Nutritional Information: 2 Servings, Amount Per Serving: Calories 220.1 Total Fat 1.4 g Saturated Fat 0.2 g Sodium 987.3 mg Total Carbohydrate 51.4 g Dietary Fiber 12.2 g Sugars 25.9 g Protein 13.9 g

Yam Chickpea Spinach Curry

I was looking for something to whip up for dinner one day and I found some frozen yams and spinach in the freezer. So I thought I'd create a different spin on *Chana Masala* with them and this is what I came up with. It's *very* hearty and *satisfying!*

Serves 2-3

Ingredients:

1 15 oz. / 425 g can of chickpeas, drained *(or 1 3/4 cups of cooked chickpeas)*

1 cup of yams, peeled and diced 2" thick

2 cups of fresh spinach, packed or 1 cup frozen, drained

2 15 oz. / 425 g cans of diced tomatoes

1 large onion, diced

3 cloves of garlic, minced

1 inch of ginger, minced

1-2 cups / 237—474 ml. vegetable broth as needed for cooking

1 tsp. roasted cumin

1 tsp. roasted coriander

1 tsp. turmeric powder

1 tsp. *Herbamare* or salt

5 tsp. sugar or sweetener *optional*

¼ tsp. *garam masala (or to taste)*

Directions:

1. Rinse canned chickpeas before using. For dried chickpeas, soak in water the night before and pressure cook with salt for 10 minutes before using.

2. In a large pan or wok, sauté onion, garlic, and ginger in vegetable broth for 5 minutes over medium heat until translucent. Add more vegetable broth if necessary, to keep from burning.

3. Add diced tomatoes and all seasonings except for *garam masala.*

4. Add chickpeas and stir to combine. Cook over medium low heat for 15 minutes, stirring occasionally, until tomatoes have broken down and chickpeas have softened. This gives the flavors a chance to blend together. Add more vegetable broth or water if the tomato juice runs low.

5. In another pot, steam the yams for 10-15 minutes until tender but retaining their shape.

6. Add spinach and stir to combine. Cook for another minute or 2 until it's wilted and heated through.

7. Add yams and stir to combine. Be careful not to break the yams apart by over mixing.

8. Serve with fresh rice and *enjoy!*

Nutrition Facts: 2 Servings, Amount Per Serving: Calories 368.1 Total Fat 2.0 g Saturated Fat 0.0g Sodium 492.4 mg Total Carbohydrate 73.6g Dietary Fiber 12.7 g Sugars 13.7g Protein 14.4g

CHAPTER 5
Comfort Sauces, Gravies and Dips

Black Bean Dip

Black Bean dip is great served with baked tortillas, rice crackers, vegetables and nachos. You can *even* use this as a *filling* in burritos or tacos!

Serves 4

Ingredients:

2 small cloves of garlic

1 15 oz. / 425 g can black beans *('no salt')*, drained

¼ cup red onion, chopped

3 Tbsp. of mild salsa

1½ Tbsp. lime juice

2 Tbsp. fresh cilantro, chopped

1 tsp. roasted cumin

1/8 tsp. chipotle chili powder

¼ tsp. *Herbamare* or salt

Directions:

1. Add garlic to food processor and process.

2. Add remaining ingredients to processor and season to taste with chipotle, *Herbamare* or salt.

3. Process until desired texture is reached.

4. Serve and *enjoy!*

Nutrition Facts: 4 Servings Amount Per Serving Calories 95.5 Total Fat 0.8 g Saturated Fat 0.0 g Sodium 182.9 mg Total Carbohydrate 17.4 g Dietary Fiber 6.1 g Sugars 2.7 g Protein 5.5 g

The BEST Guacamole

I'm *extremely* picky with guacamole. It *must* be seasoned well and have flavor, and often, at restaurants, it's just bland. I think you'll agree that this version of guacamole *has all the others beat!*

Serves 4

Ingredients:

1 large ripe avocado

1 small onion, diced

1 medium tomato, diced

1-2 cloves garlic, minced

1 large lime juiced

1 heaping tsp. roasted cumin

½ tsp. *Herbamare* or salt

¼ cup cilantro, diced

Directions:

1. Slice and de-seed the avocado. In a bowl or container, mash the avocado well with a fork.

2. Add other ingredients and combine.

3. Start with 1 clove of garlic. Add another if desired.

4. Serve and enjoy!

Nutrition Facts: 4 Servings, Amount Per Serving: Calories 101.8 Total Fat 6.8 g Saturated Fat 0.95 Sodium 298.8 mg Total Carbohydrate 12.2 g Dietary Fiber 3.85 g Sugars 1.2 g Protein 1.7 g

Cheezy Sauce for Steamed Vegetables

Growing up we often had homemade cheese sauce on our vegetables. I wanted to create a *healthier* alternative for those who *still* love a little cheezy flavor with their steamed broccoli!

Serves 4

Ingredients:

1 cup / 237 ml. almond milk *(original, unsweetened)*

¼ cup nutritional yeast flakes

¼ tsp. smoked Spanish paprika

½ tsp. miso paste *(Genmai brown rice)*

Fresh ground pepper *(if desired)*

1½ Tbsp. flour or cornstarch *(Gluten free flour if desired)*

Directions:

1. Add almond milk to a saucepan and heat over medium heat *(medium low on a gas stove)* until warm. Sprinkle in the nutritional yeast and smoked paprika. Whisk it in until blended.

2. Add miso paste, breaking it up so there are no large clumps. Heat it through while blending with the whisk. Taste, and then add more smoked paprika and ground pepper if desired. Adding more miso will make it saltier so use caution. *(You want a tangy zesty flavor)*

3. Gently sprinkle in the flour and whisk to combine, ensuring there are no clumps. Heat mixture for a minute or two until thickened. Stir to prevent sticking or burning at the bottom.

4. Turn off the stove and cover to keep warm until veggies are ready.

5. Drizzle over vegetables and serve. Keep extra aside for those dinner guests who just have to have more!

Variations:

Feel free to use soymilk, rice milk, hemp milk, etc. as desired.

Genmai brown rice miso (the type, not a brand) is important in making faux cheese. It is much tangier than white or yellow miso. I find Genmai miso gives the best results. You can buy miso at any health store in the refrigerated soy/fake meat section.

To change some flavors in this sauce, omit the smoked paprika and add garlic and onion granules - or add some Tabasco or chipotle chili powder to spice it up!

Nutrition Facts: 4 Servings, Amount Per Serving: Calories 52.4 Total Fat 1.2 g Saturated Fat 0.1 g Sodium 78.7 mg Total Carbohydrate 6.6 g Dietary Fiber 2.3 g Sugars 0.1 g Protein 4.8 g

Classic Brown Gravy

This is the gravy recipe I use on my *Garlic Mashed Potatoes* to simulate regular beef gravy.

Serves 4

Ingredients:

2 cups / 474 ml. vegetable broth *(low sodium)*

2 Tbsp. low sodium soy sauce *(or gluten free tamari)*

½ tsp. garlic powder

½ tsp. onion powder

1 tsp. maple syrup *(or liquid sweetener)*

2 Tbsp. nutritional yeast

3 Tbsp. cornstarch or flour mixed with 3 Tbsp. of water *(to make cornstarch slurry)*

Fresh ground pepper to taste

Directions:

1. Add vegetable broth, soy sauce, garlic powder, onion powder and maple syrup to a saucepan. Warm over medium heat.

2. Add the nutritional yeast and stir.

3. Taste. Add fresh ground pepper if desired.

4. Add the cornstarch slurry and whisk in. Heat for 2-4 minutes until it thickens. If you like your gravy very thick you can whisk in another 1 Tbsp. of flour mixed with 1 Tbsp. of water at the end.

5. Serve and *enjoy!*

Nutrition Facts: 4 Servings, Amount Per Serving: Calories 53.2 Total Fat 0.3 g Saturated Fat 0.1 g Sodium 371.5 mg Total Carbohydrate 9.7 g Dietary Fiber 1.7 g Sugars 2 g Protein 3.2 g

Herbed Tofu Ranch Dip

This recipe is for my Mom who absolutely *loves* Ranch dip. She missed having it with veggies on a vegan diet. I created this guilt-free version so *everyone* can enjoy a creamy dip without the dairy *or* the fat!

Serves 4

Ingredients:

1 12.3 oz. / 349 g package firm silken tofu *(like mori-nu)*

2 Tbsp. lemon juice

1 clove of garlic

1 tsp. granulated onion

½ tsp. nutritional yeast

2 tsp. maple syrup or liquid sweetener

¼ tsp. *Herbamare* or salt

Fresh ground pepper

1 Tbsp. parsley, chopped

2 Tbsp. green/spring onions, sliced *(green tops only)*

Directions:

1. Place ingredients *(except for parsley and green onions)* into blender or *Vitamix* and blend until smooth. Taste and adjust salt and pepper if desired. Add parsley and green onions and blend on medium high until the pieces are broken up a bit.

2. Refrigerate if desired before serving. Serve with veggies or rice crackers.

   Nutrition Facts: 4 Servings, Amount Per Serving: Calories 75.3 Total Fat 2.4 g Saturated Fat 0.4 g Sodium 202.3 mg Total Carbohydrate 7.7 g Dietary Fiber 0.2 g Sugars 5.3 g Protein 6.2 g

Hummus (low fat)

Most often hummus contains *loads* of oil and is pretty high in fat. This version *skips* the oil, but still retains all the delicious flavor of hummus that you love!

Serves 4

Ingredients:

1 15 oz. / 425 g can chickpeas *("no salt")* or 1¾ cup of fresh cooked chickpeas

1-2 small cloves of garlic *(depending on how spicy you like it)*

1-1/2 Tbsp. water *(this replaces the oil)*

3-4 Tbsp. lemon juice *(to taste)*

1½ Tbsp. tahini

¼ tsp. Herbamare or salt *(none if using salted canned chickpeas)*

Fresh ground pepper to taste **optional*

Directions:

1. Rinse the chickpeas—or drain if they are fresh cooked—and set aside.

2. Add garlic clove(s) to the food processor and pulse until chopped.

3. Add chickpeas, filtered water, lemon juice *(start with less and add more if desired)* and pulse until the chickpeas are blended. Taste and add more lemon if desired.

4. Add tahini, *Herbamare (if desired)* and a little fresh ground pepper. Process until everything's creamy. Taste and adjust with additional salt, pepper, lemon or water for consistency.

5. Serve with veggies, pitas, or baked chips. *Enjoy!*

Nutrition Facts: 4 Servings, Amount Per Serving: Calories 113.6 Total Fat 3.4 g Saturated Fat 0.4 g Sodium 181.8 mg Total Carbohydrate 17.7 g Dietary Fiber 5.9 g Sugars 0.3 g Protein 5.6 g

Miso Tahini Gravy

I serve this *'oh so savory'* gravy with my tasty *Herbed Lentil Loaf.* It's also the perfect partner to a batch of baked potato wedges and livens up 'every day' mashed potatoes too.

Serves 4

Ingredients:

Directions:

3 Tbsp. miso *(Genmai brown rice)*

3 Tbsp. tahini

1 cup / 237 ml. vegetable broth *(low sodium)*

1½ - 2 Tbsp. maple syrup or liquid sweetener

½ tsp. apple cider vinegar

½ tsp. garlic powder

½ tsp. onion powder

Fresh ground pepper

1 tsp. cornstarch mixed with 1 Tbsp. water *(to make cornstarch slurry)*

1. Add vegetable broth, miso, and tahini to a saucepan. Stir to break up the miso, and then heat over medium low heat.

2. Add maple syrup, apple cider vinegar, garlic powder, and onion powder. Taste, and add fresh ground pepper or any additional seasoning if desired.

3. Add cornstarch slurry and stir to combine. Heat until it thickens a bit.

4. Add enough liquid to desired consistency, heat gently but don't boil it *(this kills the beneficial culture in the miso paste.)*

5. Serve and *enjoy!*

Nutrition Facts: 4 Servings, Amount Per Serving: Calories 105.4 Total Fat 6.2 g Saturated Fat 1.0 g Sodium 78.8 mg Total Carbohydrate 11.4 g Dietary Fiber 1.4 g Sugars 6.9 g Protein 2.1 g

Roasted Baba Ganoush

If you love hummus you *have* to try *Baba Ghanoush.* It's lighter and *very* creamy and you can use it just like hummus as a dip for almost *anything!*

Serves 4

Ingredients:

1 large eggplant or about 4 baby ones *(1½ lb. / 680 g)*

2 cloves of garlic

1 1/2 Tbsp. tahini

3-4 Tbsp. lemon juice

¾ tsp. *Herbamare* or salt

½ tsp. roasted ground cumin

Directions:

1. Preheat oven to 400° F / 205° C. Pierce eggplant all over with a fork.

2. Roast in oven for 50-60 minutes until soft, and eggplant looks deflated.

3. Let cool thoroughly before touching.

4. Cut the eggplant open, scoop out the flesh, and set it aside.

5. Add the garlic to a food processor or *Vitamix* and pulse chop.

6. Add the eggplant and rest of the ingredients and combine in the food processor until smooth.

7. Season to taste with salt and pepper as desired. *Enjoy!*

Nutrition Facts: 4 Servings, Amount Per Serving: Calories 70.2 Total Fat 2.3g Saturated Fat 0.3 g Sodium 264.6 mg Potassium 392.7 mg Total Carbohydrate 12.3 g Dietary Fiber 4.5 g Sugars 0.3 g Protein 2.5 g

Rich Mushroom Gravy

I wanted to create a creamy mushroom gravy to use for all occasions and this is what I came up with. Again, it can be served with mashed potatoes, or *Herbed Lentil Loaf*—or anywhere *else* you'd like gravy!

Serves 4

Ingredients:

1 Tbsp. miso *(Genmai brown rice)*
1 Tbsp. light soy sauce *(or gluten free tamari)*
2 Tbsp. nutritional yeast

¼ cup dried mushrooms, diced
Fresh ground pepper to taste
1 Tbsp. cornstarch or flour mixed with 1 Tbsp. / 15 ml. water *(to make cornstarch slurry)*

Directions:

1. Combine all the ingredients except *slurry* in small saucepan and simmer for 5 minutes. Do not boil as this will kill the beneficial bacteria in miso.

2. Add *slurry* a little at a time, stirring constantly until thickened.

3. Serve and *enjoy!*

Nutrition Facts: 4 Servings, Amount Per Serving: Calories 44.2 Total Fat 0.3 g Saturated Fat 0.1 g Sodium 178.4 mg Total Carbohydrate 7.4 g Dietary Fiber 2.5 g Sugars 1.9 g Protein 2.4 g

Roasted Red Pepper Hummus

When you're tired of having the same old hummus, why not mix it up by adding *savory roasted red peppers*? Look for roasted red peppers in jars near the canned tomatoes at the grocery store.

Serves 8

Ingredients:

2 15 oz. / 425 g cans chickpeas *(no-salt)*

3-4 Tbsp. tahini

12 oz. / 340 g jar roasted red peppers, drained

1 - 1 ½ lemons, juiced

3-4 cloves of garlic or 1 tsp. granulated garlic powder

¼ -½ tsp. fresh ground pepper

¼ tsp. *Herbamare* or salt, or to taste

Directions:

1. Combine all ingredients in a food processor starting with the lower amount of seasonings and blend until smooth.

2. Taste test and adjust seasonings to taste and blend again if desired.

3. Serve with veggies, pita or rice crackers.

4. *Enjoy!*

Nutrition Facts: 8 servings, Amount Per Serving: Calories 163.6 Total Fat 3.9g Saturated Fat 0.4g Sodium 273.6mg Total Carbohydrate 24.9g Dietary Fiber 4.9g Sugars 2.5 g Protein 7.1 g

Southern White Gravy

A *salute to the south* with this one! I worked *days* to create a suitable, *veganized* version of your classic gravy for biscuits.

Serves 4

Ingredients:

1 cup / 237 ml. almond milk, unsweetened original

2 Tbsp. cornstarch or flour

2 tsp. nutritional yeast

1/8 tsp. *Herbamare* or salt

white pepper to taste

Directions:

1. Add almond milk to a saucepan and heat over medium low heat. Gently sprinkle in flour and whisk in quickly. Keep whisking until there are no lumps.

2. Add the nutritional yeast and whisk again.

NOTE: You won't taste the nutritional yeast. It adds a deeper flavor, making the gravy more savory.

3. Season the gravy with salt and pepper.

4. Heat gently for a few minutes until the mixture thickens. Whisk when necessary.

If you'd like thicker gravy, add another 1/2-1 Tbsp. of flour.

5. Serve and *enjoy!*

Nutrition Facts: 4 Servings, Amount Per Serving: Calories 29.8 Total Fat 0.9 g Saturated Fat 0.0 g Sodium 130.5 mg Total Carbohydrate 4.2 g Dietary Fiber 0.7 g Sugars 0.0 g Protein 1.4 g

White Bean and Thyme Gravy

This thick, savory bean gravy adds a satisfying jolt of protein to mashed potatoes, or over roasted root vegetables. The fresh thyme makes this an *especially delicious* gravy!

Serves 8

Ingredients:

1 small onion, diced

4 cloves of garlic, minced

2½ cups / 592.5 ml. vegetable broth *(low sodium)*

2½ Tbsp. fresh thyme, destemmed and chopped

1 15 oz. / 425 g can no-salt cannellini beans,

drained *(or 1 ¾ cups cooked)*

2 Tbsp. of water

¼ cup flour *(or gluten free flour)*

2½ Tbsp. light soy sauce or *(gluten free tamari)*

¼ tsp. Fresh ground pepper

Directions:

1. In a pan, sauté onions and garlic in ½ cup of broth over medium heat for 5 minutes.

2. Add thyme and cook for another 2-3 minutes.

3. Add broth to blender. Add beans and soy sauce then blend them all together.

4. Add onions and blend again.

5. Add flour and blend again.

6. Heat over medium heat, stirring occasionally, until thickened.

7. Serve and *enjoy!*

Nutrition Facts: 8 Servings, Amount Per Serving: Calories 53.3 Total Fat 0.3 g Saturated Fat 0.0 g Sodium 234.1 mg Total Carbohydrate 9.9 g Dietary Fiber 2.0 g Sugars 0.7 g Protein 2.5 g

Zesty Queso Sauce

Use this queso sauce for *all* your favorite Mexican and Tex-Mex recipes! It's featured in several recipes in this book like *Rainbow Nachos* and *Yam & Black Bean Enchiladas*.

Serves 4

Ingredients:

2/3 cup / 158 ml. canned fire roasted tomatoes *(use part of 1 can)*

1 cup / 237 ml. filtered water

½ tsp. onion powder

¼ tsp. smoked paprika

¼ tsp. garlic powder

5 Tbsp. nutritional yeast

1/8 tsp. ml. salt

Fresh ground pepper

3 Tbsp. all purpose flour or corn starch

1/8 tsp. xanthan gum *(this helps thicken and hold it together)*

Diced jalapeños / chipotle / chili powder *optional

Directions:

1. Combine tomatoes, water, onion powder, smoked paprika, garlic powder, and nutritional yeast in a blender or food processor and process until smooth—season to taste with salt and pepper. Add flour or cornstarch, and xanthan gum and blend again.

2. Pour mixture into a pot and heat over medium heat until the sauce thickens.

3. Add additional spices if desired such as: diced jalapeños, chipotle or chili powder etc.

4. Serve with baked tortilla chips, on enchiladas, in burritos, or use as a topping for baked potatoes.

5. Store leftovers in a container in the fridge. Use within 3-5 days.

Nutrition Facts: 4 Servings (1/2 C each), Amount Per Serving: Calories 48.5 Total Fat 0.2 g Saturated Fat 0.0 g Sodium 74.2 mg Total Carbohydrate 8.8 g Dietary Fiber 1.7 g Sugars 0.0 g Protein 2.2 g

CHAPTER 6
Bonus Recipes

Easy Sautéed Mushrooms

These are based on my Mom's sautéed mushrooms. We put them in *everything:* mashed potatoes, on top of burgers, in tofu omelets, in tacos etc. I love adding minced garlic or onions to these. Use *your* imagination!

Serves 2

Ingredients:

2 cups / 474 ml. mushrooms, sliced

1 Tbsp. low sodium soy sauce *(or Gluten free tamari)*

½ Tbsp. brown sugar

1 Tbsp. water

Directions:

1. Heat a pan over medium heat and add soy sauce and brown sugar. Use a spatula to combine.

2. Add water and mushrooms and cook for 6-8 minutes until soft and shrunken.

Variations:

Add 1 tsp. of fresh minced ginger, or garlic, for an even *more savory* recipe!

Nutrition Facts: 2 Servings, Amount Per Serving: Calories 37.1 Total Fat 0.2 g Saturated Fat 0.0 g Sodium 304.6 mg Total Carbohydrate 9.0 g Dietary Fiber 0.9 g Sugars 7.3 g Protein 2.6 g

Fat Free Vegan Two Bite Banana Brownies

Sometimes you want to—have to—*need to!*—have a bite of something chocolaty! Make these when you're craving a wee taste of dessert, and then freeze the rest for *later!*

Makes 24 mini muffin tin brownies

Ingredients:

½ cup plus 3 Tbsp. whole-wheat flour *(or Gluten free, see NOTE)*

½ cup brown sugar

¼ cup cocoa powder, unsweetened

1¼ tsp. baking powder

½ tsp. salt

½ Tbsp. ground chia or flax seed

2 Tbsp. water

½ cup plus 3 Tbsp. ripe mashed bananas *(about 2 large)* or applesauce

1 Tbsp. vanilla extract

Non-stick cooking spray

NOTE: If using Gluten Free flour, add ¼ tsp. of xanthan gum to help the batter stick together.

Directions:

1. Preheat oven to 325° F / 163° C
2. Combine dry ingredients, except brown sugar and chia in a medium sized bowl.
3. Add 2 Tbsp. water to a small bowl. Shake in ground chia and stir until combined.
4. Add wet ingredients and brown sugar to another bowl and stir in chia.
5. Add wet ingredients to dry ingredients and stir until mixed.
6. Spray a mini muffin tin with non-stick spray.
7. Spoon a tsp. size amount into each cup, filling about ¾ full.
8. Bake for 15-16 minutes, or until done in the center when you check with a toothpick.
9. Let brownies cool in the pan for 10-15 minutes.
10. Remove and place on wire rack to finish cooling.

Additional Tips:

Really ripe bananas are best for this as they're sweeter and add depth—the same as you'd use for banana bread.

If you substitute applesauce the brownies will have less flavor, so you might want to add more sweetener.

These brownies are easily frosted or glazed.

Freeze a batch in freezer bags for a quick treat ready to go.

Nutrition Facts: Per brownie, Amount Per Serving: Calories 38.5 Total Fat 0.2 g Saturated Fat 0.1 g Sodium 76.0 mg Total Carbohydrate 10.6 g Dietary Fiber 0.9 g Sugars 6.9 g Protein 0.7 g

Rice Pudding

My Mom's friend started talking about how much she *loved* the homemade rice pudding she had as a child. Of course, then we *all* started to crave it! So, I went into the kitchen and whipped up this vegan rice pudding that ended up satisfying *everyone!*

Serves 8

Ingredients:

4 cups / 1 qt. / 0.95 L almond milk *(unsweetened original)*

1 cup / 118 ml water

1 cup long grain white rice

1/4 cup raisins

1/2 cup sugar or maple syrup

2 tsp. vanilla extract

Cinnamon *(for garnish)*

NOTE: Brown rice takes TWICE as long to cook as white rice. If you use brown rice you will need to cook your pudding for 45-50 minutes over the stovetop.

1. Combine almond milk, water, rice and raisins in a saucepan and carefully bring to a boil and then reduce heat to low.

2. Cook for 20-25 minutes until rice is soft and liquid is absorbed.

3. Add vanilla and sugar and stir to combine.

4. Cook for another few minutes until sugar dissolves.

5. Remove from heat and let thicken.

6. Serve warm or chilled in bowls and garnish with cinnamon.

Directions - *Zojirushi/Advanced Fuzzy Logic* Rice Cookers:

1. Combine ingredients except for cinnamon in rice cooker pan and stir.

2. Set to porridge setting and cook.

3. Serve warm or chilled in bowls and garnish with cinnamon.

Directions - Pressure Cooker:

1. Add milk to pressure cooker, bring to a boil.

2. Stir in the rice.

3. Close lid and turn to high heat and bring up to high pressure.

4. Lower the heat and cook at continuous pressure for 10 minutes.

5. Remove from heat.

6. Release pressure with the natural release method letting the pressure drop of its own accord.

7. Unlock lid and stir in sugar, vanilla and raisins.

8. Serve warm or chilled in bowls and garnish with cinnamon.

Additional Tips:

If you like a very thick dry rice pudding you can omit the cup of water.

Nutritional Info: 8 servings, Calories: 164.4 Total Fat 1.3 g Sat Fat 0 g Sodium 69.3 mg Carbohydrates 35.5 g Fiber 0.8 g Sugars 15.3 g Protein 2.2 g

Enjoy, Enjoy, ENJOY!
Yours, Veronica Grace

Note from the Author

Thank you for purchasing this book! I hope I have inspired you and your family to try some healthier versions of your favorite Comfort Foods! I believe that my dishes should taste great as well as being healthy, so they were designed with you in mind. If you're transitioning to a vegan or low fat, plant based diet, or looking for dishes to serve to your omnivore family, these recipes will help you succeed in your journey!

Please feel free to contact me via email veronica@lowfatveganchef.com or my blog (LowFatVeganChef.com)—and make sure you sign up for my newsletter to get my free 'Recipe of the Week'!

If you enjoyed these recipes you may also enjoy my other recipe books:

Comfort Soups to Keep You Warm

Featuring over 30 delicious homemade soup recipes, all oil-free and low in fat, but full of flavor! Some favorites include: "Just Like" Chicken Noodle Soup, Roasted Butternut Squash Soup, Mexican Black Bean Corn Soup, Creamy Potato Corn Chowder, Gourmet Cream of Mushroom Soup and many more!

http://www.lowfatveganchef.com/comfortsoups

Simply Decadent Smoothies

Features over 50 fruit and green smoothie recipes. Learn how to design your own smoothies using whole fruits and greens without fillers such as sugar, dairy, or sorbets. 100% natural and 100% good for you!

http://www.lowfatveganchef.com/simplysmoothies

Savory Raw Dinner Recipes

Features 55 raw vegan recipes you can use for appetizers, entrees and snacks. It focuses on whole raw plant foods and shows you how to make your own raw blended soups, homemade salad dressings, dehydrated crackers, chips and tortilla wraps, as well as entrees such as raw lasagna, raw chili and more!

http://www.lowfatveganchef.com/savory

Index

Index

Index

CPSIA information can be obtained at www.ICGtesting.com
Printed in the USA
LVOW020943070513

332613LV00002B/2/P